CALIFORNIA

LIVING + EATING

This book is dedicated to my father, Richard Anthony Maidment, who taught me many things, but especially to love good food and to love California.

PHOTOGRAPHY BY
NASSIMA ROTHACKER

CALIFORNIA

LIVING + EATING

Recipes Inspired by the Golden State

ELEANOR MAIDMENT

Hardie Grant

BOOKS

CONTENTS

What has always struck me about Californian food is its freshness. Not just in its produce, but in the beautiful presentation, the boldness in experimenting with flavours and the innovative fusion-style of cooking that has evolved from an ethnically diverse population. Driven by seasonality and fresh produce, it is effortlessly healthy, with an openness, freeness and modernity that I haven't witnessed anywhere else. It is an approach to eating that I find both inspirational and aspirational.

INTRODUCTION

When I first conceived the idea of writing a cookbook inspired by California, I did not fully understand the depth and complexity of what is meant by the term 'California cuisine'.

I have never lived in the States, I don't claim to be an expert on California cuisine and this book is not aiming to be a bible of its food. But having visited regularly over the last three decades, I have watched its food scene evolve and blossom into something quite unique. This book has been a wonderful opportunity to express how California inspires me. The recipes are all my own, merging my experience as a food writer with some of the bright, innovative ideas I have absorbed while travelling the West Coast. My simple aim is to enhance and invigorate the way people cook at home. Having grown up in the UK at a time when traditional European cuisines were considered king, it has been interesting to look at a cuisine that has really only existed for 50 years. That youth and vivacity is something we can all benefit from in the kitchen.

WHY CALIFORNIA?

My first trip to California was in the late 1980s and I returned almost every summer until my late teens. Looking back, my memories are as much shaped by where and what I ate, as the trips to Disneyland or Universal Studios.

By the early 1990s, the reason for the frequent visits to the States was my father, an Anglo-Indian who grew up in Kolkata. After India gained independence, life for the Anglo-Indians became difficult and he moved with my grandparents to the UK in 1959, aged 15. For as long as I can remember he was fascinated by the idea of the American dream. His own personal experiences, perhaps of neither feeling at home in India nor in the UK, shaped this vision that the US was a land of opportunity where you could come from anywhere and be anything. Having studied American government and politics at LSE, in London, he went on to be a professor in the subject, and subsequently my early life was heavily influenced by my truly Americophile parent.

During his career, my father made a series of documentaries for the Open University looking at the success of immigrant communities in the States. I vividly recall one summer accompanying him at various filming locations in LA, each focusing on a different community, from traditional Japanese bakers in Little Tokyo to the philanthropic Jews of Beverly Hills. We travelled extensively in the state, we ate well, and we spent a lot of time with first- and second-generation Californians of various different backgrounds.

My fascination with culture and food is very much formed by these early experiences and by my own mixed heritage, growing up in London to parents of Jewish and Anglo-Indian descent, two cultures that hold food very dearly. My mother has lived in Israel since the late 1990s and, there too, the rich ethnic tapestry and the way it is expressed in its food has always charmed me. This fascination remained as I finished school, travelled extensively, went to university to study social anthropology and wrote my dissertation on the cultural inheritance of food.

I began my career as a food writer shortly after graduating in 2003. But it was really after training at Leiths School of Food and Wine in London, and then becoming the food editor of high-end supermarket *Waitrose Food* magazine, that my professional life began to revolve around ideas to inspire home cooks. My mind whirred constantly with clever ways to teach people how to elevate their home cooking. And, again, I found myself making regular trips to the West Coast for fresh ideas. But why, when there are so many places to spark that culinary creativity, have I always been drawn to California?

Firstly, it is important to remember that most world cuisines are firmly rooted in history. At Leiths the techniques we learned were mainly French. When we cook Italian food there's almost a competitive urge to make it as classic as possible, and with most Asian food we aim to recreate dishes that have been home-cooked the same way for generations.

Not with California cuisine: its roots are in the future, it moves with the times and it is constantly evolving. The term 'California cuisine' was only really coined in the early 1970s and that period was integral in shaping the food scene that exists there today. A lot of insight into this subject came from American chef and writer, Joyce Goldstein, author of *Inside the California Food Revolution*. She was kind enough to let me interview her for this book, and I am forever grateful to her.

FARM-TO-TABLE + SELF-TAUGHT CHEFS

The 1970s saw the arrival of some key chefs in the Bay Area of San Francisco, who went on to create what is now known as California cuisine. The most widely recognised of them is Alice Waters of Chez Panisse, an iconic Berkeley restaurant that opened in 1971. If you look at Chez Panisse's menu, it might be hard to understand why it is heralded as a great Californian restaurant. Dishes such as shellfish consommé and berry clafoutis are undeniably influenced by France and the Mediterranean.

But that's because chefs like Waters and her contemporaries travelled extensively learning the great cuisines of Europe. They were hugely inspired by the amount of fresh, ripe produce they ate across the Mediterranean. At that time, the mind-blowing kaleidoscope of fruit and veg that you see at farmers' markets up and down California today did not exist. So, on their return they forged relationships with farmers, initiating the planting and cultivating of all the wonderful produce they had experienced abroad. These burgeoning relationships between farmer and chef – and the intertwining of their two fates – created the birth of the farm-to-table movement. And, like the crops they planted, it blossomed quickly. The deserts, wetlands, endless coastline and year-round sunshine made California a fertile ground for growing just about anything. Today chefs continue to work closely with farmers, and because of the abundance of raw ingredients, Californians are completely obsessed with 'locally grown'.

These self-taught chefs (many of whom, incidentally, were female) concentrated on the flavours of the Mediterranean, completely unbound by the rules and restrictions of European training or the rigidity of tradition. They didn't have mentors correcting them on how a dish *should* be prepared, and they were free to experiment in the kitchen. Talent without boundaries can be a magical thing.

FUSION CUISINE

California's eclectic food scene was also, partly, a product of LA's diverse and ever-changing ethnic make-up. I grew up in central London, which I consider to be a fairly culturally diverse upbringing, but LA is something else entirely. I clearly remember the much-loved food writer, the late Jonathan Gold, in his brilliant documentary *City of Gold*, describing LA as, 'less of melting pot and more of a mosaic of culture'. It is a sprawling city of over 13 million people, where communities like Koreatown sit next to Little Tokyo, and you can eat authentic food in Little Armenia, Filipinotown and Little Arabia, and that's not to mention that almost half the population is Latino. There's no doubt that its proximity and links to Mexico have had the most significant impact on the southern Californian food scene.

While these ethnic hubs in the most part sit separately, with defined boundaries, a culinary osmosis occurred over time, as cooks started to borrow from each other. And it's in Los Angeles that fusion cuisine started to shine in a way that had never been seen before.

When I started working for a London restaurant guide in 2003, 'fusion' had already become a negative word, and indeed there are endless examples of bad culinary mergers. But it would be remiss not to look at some of the beautiful examples that were born in LA, where, because of its unique demographic, a chef can instinctively understand and respect two cuisines that have so little in common, and adapt, imitate and combine the best bits of each of them to great effect. You see fusion in menus all over California today – creatively borrowing and lending – and it's often executed with the daring and respect it deserves. It goes against a lot of what I've been taught in my career. But, again, it is that 'no rules' Californian approach that I love. Good food is simply good food, no matter where it comes from.

California Living + Eating

HEALTHY EATING

Another important aspect of California cuisine that many people immediately identify with is a focus on health, particularly given the explosion of the wellness industry in the last five years. In the heartland of show business and entertainment, people want – need, even – to look good. Health and exercise trends come thick and fast from California, before making their way into the gyms, supermarkets and coffee shops of the rest of the world.

California was also the birthplace of the hippie movement, the counterculture that blossomed in the 1960s opposing war, fighting racism and spreading the word of peace and love. Its protagonists cared about what they ate, often adopting raw, vegan lifestyles and going to great lengths to live off the land. Back then it was perhaps more of a philosophy on food than a way to enjoy it, but it is striking how the hippie food trends of the 60s and 70s – tahini, alfalfa sprouts, brown rice and avocado toast – are now the height of fashion. In culinary terms this style of eating has come a long way.

A year before I wrote this book I studied at Matthew Kenney Culinary, a raw vegan cookery school based in Venice, LA. (At the time of publication, Matthew Kenney Culinary, or Plantlab Culinary as it later became known, will have indefinitely closed.) Matthew Kenney is a well-known plant-based chef with restaurants around the world, and it was eye-opening to see the creativity that can go into raw vegan cuisine. The techniques for preparing fruit, vegetables, nuts and seeds – and the ability to turn them into dishes that you could not conceive from the raw ingredients – were astonishing, and completely different to anything I learned at classical cookery school 10 years previously. Some of the recipes in this book are undoubtedly influenced by my time studying there. Raw vegan is in my opinion, however, a fairly extreme diet choice and certainly not representative of the whole of California. But if you want to experience and enjoy this kind of food you'd be hard-pushed to find a better place to eat it.

California Living + Eating

RECIPES INSPIRED BY THE GOLDEN STATE

All of the recipes in this book are my own interpretation of California cuisine. Some are directly inspired by dishes I have eaten on my travels, but most of them are simply intended to typify the Californian spirit. For me this spirit encompasses many themes: the love of cooking on outdoor grills, the bright and brilliant sauces to go with everything, the way that fruit makes an appearance in so many savoury dishes and the attention given to the presentation of food. But there are four main anchors that I kept coming back to while developing the recipes:

THE FREEDOM TO BREAK FROM TRADITIONAL CULINARY RULES

THE COURAGE AND UNDERSTANDING TO RESPECTFULLY FUSE DIFFERENT CUISINES

A SUB-CONSCIOUS DRIVE TOWARDS HEALTHY EATING

A CARE FOR SEASONALITY AND WELL-SOURCED PRODUCE

The question I was asked most while writing this book, is 'how can we eat the same quality of produce as in California when we don't live there?' The truth is that it may not always be possible, and we may also not have access to the huge range of fruit and vegetables. But the message is to care about your ingredients. I urge you to buy from a farmers' market, or a shop where you trust and know the provenance of the produce. And try to eat seasonally, as it truly makes a huge difference to flavour. I understand the financial restraints around eating that we all face, but the ingredients I use are not luxurious or prohibitively expensive. There is, unquestionably, a difference in taste if you invest time on sourcing good produce and eating high-welfare meat and fish. It may not be possible to have quite the same 'eat local' approach as Californians, but the ethos is something we can all strive towards.

This book is also more about eating with a 'healthful approach' than about prescribed notions of 'healthy eating'. I don't exclude food types, as I believe an inclusive diet – eating as wide a range of unprocessed foods as possible – is the key to good health. Californians put as much emphasis on vegetables as they do on meat and seafood, and I think it's a balanced and wise way to think about what you're putting on your plate.

During my eight years as the food editor of *Waitrose Food* magazine, I developed hundreds of realistic and achievable recipes for our readers. Some of the recipes in this book take 20 minutes, others longer, but all are designed to be accessible to the home cook, and I have tried my best to give instructions that are as detailed and explanatory as possible.

As a food writer, researching this book, travelling in one of my favourite places in the world and taking culinary inspiration from somewhere that positively brims with creativity has been a huge pleasure. In Europe, perhaps worldwide, I feel that California doesn't always get the acknowledgement it deserves for its influence on the global food scene. I hope this book helps shift that, even in a small way. And I hope it encourages you to eat well, every day, just like they do in California.

CULINARY INSPIRATION THAT BRIMS WITH CREATIVITY

COOKS' NOTES

My aim when writing this book was to make the recipes as accessible as possible, using as few unusual or hard-to-source ingredients and as little exclusive equipment as possible. I have tested all the recipes myself at least twice, often many more times, and several have been cooked by some very kind friends to whom I am forever grateful. I have tried to be as precise and descriptive as possible with ingredients and methods, but cooking is not an exact science. Produce, equipment and kitchen environments can vary greatly, so treat the recipes as a guide and remember to trust your instincts.

—

INGREDIENTS

Butter – I always use unsalted butter in cooking. I prefer to add my own salt.

Eggs – I always use medium, room temperature eggs (though the size of eggs is only really relevant in baking when variations can make a difference).

Ginger – All ginger is peeled unless otherwise specified. Peeling it using a teaspoon is by far the easiest way. And try organic ginger if you come across it, it has more fire than mass-farmed varieties.

Meat + Poultry – Try not to cook meat and poultry straight from the fridge. Let it sit for about 30 minutes at room temperature before cooking. It will reduce the overall cooking time and give more even results (as the internal temperature will rise more in line with the external temperature).

Nuts + Seeds – I use a lot of nuts and seeds in recipes and they are shelled and unsalted unless otherwise specified. I frequently roast/toast nuts and have given general instructions for this on page 25.

Olive Oil – Use good-quality extra-virgin olive oil for dressings and as a seasoning to drizzle over dishes before serving. Use milder olive oils for cooking.

Onions + Garlic – These are always peeled unless otherwise specified.

Salt – I like to use flaky sea salt in most savoury recipes (Maldon is my preferred brand) and fine sea salt in most baking and sweet recipes (and I really do think that all sweet recipes benefit from a pinch of salt). I tend to layer up salt, adding a little at each stage of cooking. I think it gives more depth to the finished dish.

Seasoning to Taste – Constantly taste your food and season it as you go along. With your final taste, consider what the dish needs to balance out the flavours. I just as often finish dishes with a squeeze of lemon juice as I do salt; when used together, salt and acid are very good at prising flavour out of food. Also bear in mind that a little sweetness can balance savoury. And don't disregard other ingredients that are used to finish dishes around the globe – fish sauce, soy sauce, honey, toasted sesame oil, lime, fresh chilli, chilli flakes, salty cheese, pomegranate seeds, toasted cumin seeds and all sorts of other spices – there's a world of seasoning out there just waiting to be explored.

Vanilla Bean Paste –Generally I use vanilla bean paste rather than extract as it is thicker and contains bean powder, giving lovely flecks of vanilla in the finished dish.

Water – Don't be afraid to treat water as an ingredient. It is essential in helping to achieve the right consistency in soups and sauces and it can help to slow down the cooking process when it's moving too fast. Also, if a sauce or stew is lacking depth, you may just need to simmer off a little of the excess water to concentrate the flavour.

Yeast – Throughout this book I have used easy bake yeast (you can usually buy this in tubs or pre-measured 7 g/¼ oz sachets), as different types can vary. If your dough doesn't rise, there can be a number of reasons. Firstly, it's worth checking the yeast has not expired. If it has, try mixing the yeast in some lukewarm liquid (usually milk or water) with a teaspoon of sugar and leave it for 5 minutes. If it froths up, then the yeast is active and you can add this to the recipe with the wet ingredients. It's also worth remembering that yeast is greatly affected by temperature. On cold days, dough can take double the amount of time to rise as it does on a hot day.

EQUIPMENT

Blenders + Food Processors – Blenders and food processors are different things, and I think it's worth having both in your kitchen. Blenders finely whizz foods like soups and sauces, while food processors offer a more rough chop and are brilliant for making pestos and pastry. In my opinion, NutriBullet make very good value high-speed blenders (though you can only blend small volumes at a time). Magimix are my go-to for food processors.

Digital Scales – Invest in a set of digital scales. They're inexpensive and make baking (and all your cooking) much more precise. I tend to weigh water and similar viscosity liquids using the ml function on my digital scales as it's more precise.

Electric Beaters – I couldn't live without these for cake-making. They're great for creaming butter, whisking egg whites and whipping up buttercreams and frostings.

Graters + Zesters – Microplane make a brilliant range of graters. If you don't own at least one already, you will be pleased when you do. They're great for zesting citrus, as well as grating cheeses.

Hand-held Stick Blenders – I didn't own a hand-held blender until I discovered that they make mayonnaise in seconds. Now I can't live without one. They're also really useful for blending soups and they often come with mini food processor attachments, which are useful for making small quantities of things like salsa and pesto.

Julienne Peeler – A small, inexpensive and useful piece of equipment for quickly shredding carrots and other root vegetables.

Knives – Get rid of any blunt knives, they're a waste of space. All most cooks need is one good-quality and regularly sharpened 18 cm (7 in) or 20 cm (8 in) chef's knife and one smaller serrated knife for cutting tomatoes and chillies. A decent bread knife is a good investment, too. I think Sabatier makes excellent value knives (you don't need to spend much more than £30), and I would suggest visiting a specialist knife shop if you want to invest more.

Mandoline – A mandoline is extremely useful for finely slicing vegetables. I use mine regularly, though mandolines are extremely sharp and should always be used with care.

Ovens – All ovens vary in their cooking temperatures so you need to get to know yours, check the manufacturer's instructions and, if necessary, use an oven thermometer. The recipes in this book have been tested in a fan-assisted oven at the given temperatures, but these should be treated as a guide only. If you are cooking in a conventional, non-fan-assisted oven, you should increase the temperatures by 10–20 °C (50–60 °F).

Pots + Pans – I own just a few, good-quality saucepans, frying pans (skillets) and casseroles (Dutch ovens) all with lids and in different sizes. I invested in them, I look after them and they will last a lifetime. I also have two ovenproof sauté pans (26 cm/10 in and 28 cm/11 in) with tight-fitting lids and use them all the time.

Spoon Measures – Tablespoon (15 ml), dessertspoon (10 ml) and teaspoon (5 ml) measures are exact quantities and cannot be replicated with cutlery spoons. Unless specified as 'heaped' or 'scant', spoon measures are level. Use a knife or your finger to level off the top.

Stand Mixers – These are different to food processors and usually come with a much higher price tag. I find them fairly ineffective for whisking smaller quantities of eggs whites and beating cake batters as the attachments rarely seem to reach the bottom of the bowl. But if you are serious about making breads and yeasted pastries, a stand mixer with a dough hook is your best friend.

Your Nose, Your Hands + Your Ears – There's plenty of great equipment that can make us better cooks, but do learn to trust your own senses, too. When you start to smell something in the oven it's often an indicator that it's close to being ready. Gently pressing a piece of salmon or a steak in its thickest part and feeling its firmness is a good gauge as to how well it is cooked (this, of course, takes time to learn but it does work). And you can also hear how things are cooking; if onions sizzle too loudly when they hit a pan of hot oil it's usually an indicator to turn the heat down. Our instincts go a long way in cooking, so listen to them.

A FEW LITTLE EXTRAS

Here are a few extra recipes, techniques and suggestions that will elevate your everyday eating. Some refer directly to recipes in the book, others are just simply useful to bear in mind when cooking.

—

CHARRED SOURDOUGH

I suggest serving many of the recipes in this book with toast. And when I'm entertaining guests, I find that splashing sliced sourdough with extra virgin olive oil and then charring it on a griddle and sprinkling with a little flaky sea salt makes it so much more impressive. That little bit of extra effort is so worth it: it looks lovely, adds an extra dimension of flavour and still tastes nice once it has cooled down. For garlicky toasts, rub sliced sourdough with the cut-side of a peeled and halved garlic clove before splashing with oil.

—

CHICKEN STOCK

Homemade stock is better than anything you can buy, and there's something cathartic about the delicate cooking process. If you nurture it properly, you'll taste the love in the finished stock.

Place a whole 1½ kg (3 lb 3 oz) chicken in the base of a large stock pot or casserole, with 500 g (1 lb 1 oz) chicken wings, 1 large, halved unpeeled onion, 1 halved carrot, 2 halved celery stalks, 6 black peppercorns, a bunch of parsley, 1 teaspoon of sea salt and a pinch of sugar. Cover with 3 litres (100 fl oz/12½ cups) cold water and place over a high heat. Bring to a very gentle simmer, skim any scum that rises to the surface, then turn to the lowest heat and continue to simmer as gently as possible (you want a few small bubbles coming up occasionally) for 35 minutes.

Lift the chicken out and carefully cut away the breast meat (use a chopping board placed inside a baking tray (pan) to catch any escaping juices); cool the breasts and keep for salads (see Asian-Style Chicken Salad on page 72) and sandwiches. Return the remaining whole chicken to the pot and continue to simmer gently for another 2 hours.

Skim any scum that rises to the surface throughout. Turn off the heat and cool for 1 hour, then lift out the chicken. Strain the liquid through a fine-mesh sieve (strainer) lined with a layer of paper towels into a large clean pan. Discard the wings and aromatics. Shred the meat from the legs, discarding any skin and bones.

You now have a good basic chicken stock (about 1½ litres/50 fl oz/6¼ cups), and good amount of leg meat. I would suggest turning it into Jewish Penicillin (page 148), though homemade stock will sit happily in your freezer for 3 months ready for all sorts of soups and stews.

—

HONEY NUT BUTTER

I couldn't resist putting a recipe for nut butter in this book. I remember strolling the aisles of a northern Californian supermarket in 2014 and seeing the shelves bulging with all kinds of nut butter, when in the UK we were only just getting our heads around almond butter. Now, of course, we are used to having a range of choices, but making your own puts those leftover bags of nuts lurking in the cupboard to good use.

Preheat a fan oven to 180°C (350°F/gas 6). Very roughly chop 250 g (9 oz) mixed nuts and scatter in a large, parchment-lined baking tray (pan). Roast for 5 minutes, then stir through 2 teaspoons of honey and 1½ teaspoons of flaky sea salt and return to the oven for another 3–5 minutes until deep golden. Take out of the oven and set aside. Once completely cool, whizz the nuts in a food processor until smooth. This may take a while but just leave the motor running, stopping to scrape down the sides occasionally, and you'll end up with a lovely smooth nut butter. Allow it to cool (it will have warmed in the blending process), then tip into a jar, seal and store in a dark place. The oil will naturally separate, so just stir it back in before serving.

—

LABNEH

Labneh is really just thickened yoghurt, left to strain for longer than, say, Greek yoghurt. Although we closely associate it with the Middle East, where it can be made from a number of different animal milks, there are versions to be found the world over. This is a simple mixture of cow and goat's yoghurt infused with lemon and soft herbs. You need to prepare the labneh at least a day in advance.

In a bowl, mix 450 g (1 lb/generous 1¾ cups) of natural cow's milk yoghurt and 450 g (1 lb/generous 1¾ cups) of natural goat's milk yoghurt with 2 sprigs each of fresh mint and dill, 1 teaspoon of sea salt and a pinch of caster (superfine) sugar. Using a vegetable peeler, pare the zest of 1 lemon in one long strip, then mix into the yoghurt. Line a sieve (fine-mesh strainer) with a piece of clean muslin (cheesecloth) and sit it over a mixing bowl. Tip the yoghurt mixture into the muslin, lift the corners together and tie up; put in the refrigerator and leave to sit overnight (12 hours) in the sieve over the bowl. The next day, remove the labneh from the refrigerator and discard any water that has collected in the bowl. Untie the muslin, pick out and discard the aromatics and stir up the labneh. It's now ready to serve. Try the Roasted Squash with Labneh and Zhoug on page 104.

—

PRESERVED LEMONS

Californian chefs love the Meyer lemon, a particular variety grown in southern California that is sweet, soft, thin-skinned and preserves particularly well. You can sometimes find them in the UK, but preserving any lemon is a good idea. Preparing them like this, as with most salting, was originally a technique to make foods last longer (hence 'preserved' lemons), but it's also a great way to intensify a lemon's bitter and sour qualities.

Sterilise a 1 litre jar (34 fl oz/4 cups), washing the jar and the lid in warm soapy water, then rinsing well and placing in a low fan oven (110°C/230°F/ gas ¼). Or run it through the hot cycle of your dishwasher. Wash the outside of 6 lemons in warm, soapy water, then rinse thoroughly and dry well with a clean tea (kitchen) towel. Trim the ends then cut each into quarters. Toss in a bowl with 5 tablespoons flaky sea salt, 2 fresh bay leaves and 5 black peppercorns (a cinnamon stick is nice too), then pack tightly into the jar. Squeeze the juice from another 4 lemons and pour over the top. If it doesn't cover the lemons, add enough water to cover. Seal the jar tightly and leave in a cool dark place, turning

daily. They should be ready to eat in about 3–4 weeks and once opened should be stored in the fridge. They will keep for up to 6 months.

In most cases it is the lemon rind which is used in recipes: scoop out the flesh with a teaspoon and finely slice or chop the rind into salads and stews. I think its sharpness works particularly well against richer meats and oily fish. Try the Chicken Liver Toasts with Preserved Lemon on page 135. And do experiment with eating the flesh and the preserving liquor too.

—

TOASTED NUTS + SEEDS

I use toasted nuts and seeds a lot in cooking, so thought it would be wise to give some guidelines on how best to do this. Firstly, I can't count the number of times I've burnt nuts. Because of their high fat content, they turn from a lovely shade of nutty golden to blackened and bitter in a matter of minutes. So try not to get distracted while you're in the process, and do trust your sense of smell… it's a very good indicator as to when they're done. (The same, incidentally, goes for most baking – if you can smell it, it's ready!)

Generally, I prefer to roast nuts and seeds in the oven. Their uneven shapes mean you get uneven results with dry-frying, whereas roasting gives a good all-round colour. Preheat a fan oven to 160°C (320°F/gas 4), and check them after 6 minutes. Different nuts in different ovens will take shorter or longer. Sesame seeds are the one anomaly that I prefer to toast in a dry frying pan (skillet), as they need to be tossed regularly during the toasting process.

California knows how to brunch! It may be the first meal of the day, but it's also the brightest and boldest, and pretty much anything goes. Dishes can be sweet or deeply savoury, sometimes spicy and complex, sometimes comfortingly pared back. Influences come thick and fast from around the globe, though the Mexican breakfasts are often the star of the morning show.

MORNING SUN

California Living + Eating

SERVES: 2
PREP: 15 mins
COOK: 20 mins

Translated as 'rancher's eggs', this is a simple breakfast traditionally eaten by farmers in the Mexican countryside. You'll find countless interpretations, but this is very quick and deeply satisfying considering the sum of its parts – pretty much just eggs, warm salsa and corn tortillas. I serve it with a little grated cheese, sliced avocado and a few coriander (cilantro) leaves, but I've frequently seen it with feta, pico de gallo (tomato, onion and chilli salsa), black beans and sizzling chorizo thrown into the mix.

HUEVOS RANCHEROS

400 g (14 oz) tin of good-quality
   chopped tomatoes
1 garlic clove
1 jalapeño or mild green chilli,
   roughly chopped
½ teaspoon sea salt
¼ teaspoon caster (superfine) sugar
½ teaspoon ground cumin
4 eggs
4 small corn tortillas
40 g (1½ oz) grated red Leicester
   cheese (or Cheddar)
small handful of coriander (cilantro)
   leaves, roughly chopped
½ avocado, peeled, halved and sliced

Tip the tomatoes into a small blender or food processor with the garlic, chilli (you can remove the seeds but I think the sauce needs a bit of heat), salt, sugar and cumin. Blitz until smooth, then tip into a large frying pan (skillet). Rinse out the jug with a splash of water and add the water to the pan. Bring the salsa to a simmer and cook, stirring occasionally, for 8–10 minutes. The aim is for the garlic to cook out and mellow in flavour, and the sauce to thicken.

Make 4 rough indents in the sauce with a spoon (it will still be quite loose so don't worry if they don't hold completely). Crack an egg into each indent. Cover the pan with a lid or a sheet of kitchen foil and leave to cook gently for 4–5 minutes until the egg whites are just set but the yolks are still soft.

While the eggs are cooking, toast the tortillas. I like to lay them over a naked flame on the hob until they char in places, then flip them, but you can also dry-toast them in a hot frying pan or griddle pan, or warm them in a hot oven. In this recipe I cook them for a little longer than usual so they crisp up slightly, as they'll end up softening in the sauce.

Place 2 tortillas on each plate and spoon over the eggs and salsa. Scatter over the cheese and coriander and serve with sliced avocado.

———

NOTES ON… CHILLI
Although we know certain varieties of chilli are hotter than others, it's hard to gauge the heat of a chilli without tasting it (although as a general rule, smaller tends to be hotter). I always cut off a small piece and try it before I start cooking, then I can add as little or as much as I want, seeds or no seeds, to reach the desired heat. If you choose to deseed your chillies, a great little tip I learned is to halve the chilli lengthways, then scoop out the seeds and membrane using a teaspoon.

MAKES: about
1.5 kg (3 lb 5 oz)
PREP: 20 mins
COOK: 45 mins

This is a brilliant granola, not too sweet and perfectly crisp. The joy, of course, is adapting the recipe according to whatever leftover packets of seeds, nuts and dried fruit you have in your cupboards, though this combination is particularly good and makes enough for at least 15 portions. It stores well at room temperature in an airtight container.

COCONUT JUMBO OAT GRANOLA

—

with charred stone fruit

Coconut granola
100 g (3½ oz/generous ¾ cup)
　flame or jumbo raisins
50 g (2 oz/⅓ cup) whole skin-on
　almonds, roughly chopped
50 g (2 oz/⅓ cup) shelled unsalted
　pistachios, roughly chopped
50 g (2 oz/½ cup) pecans,
　roughly chopped
250 g (9 oz/2½ cups) jumbo oats
25 g (¾ oz/scant ¼ cup)
　pumpkin seeds
25 g (¾ oz/3 tablespoons) chia seeds
4 tablespoons coconut oil
5 tablespoons maple syrup
1 teaspoon ground cinnamon
1 teaspoon vanilla bean paste
4 tablespoons water
½ teaspoon flaky sea salt
50 g (2 oz/1 cup) coconut flakes

To serve (per person)
1 nectarine, peach or apricot,
　halved and stoned
1 teaspoon melted unsalted butter
150 g (5 oz) Greek or natural yoghurt
a few edible flowers (optional)

Preheat a fan oven to 150°C (300°F/gas 3) and line a large baking tray (pan) with baking parchment. Soak the raisins in a bowl of just-boiled water while you prepare the other ingredients.

In a large mixing bowl combine the chopped nuts, oats and seeds. Put the coconut oil, maple syrup, cinnamon, vanilla and water in a small saucepan and heat until it comes to a simmer. Drain the raisins and tip them into the saucepan, then pour everything over the nuts, oat and seeds mixture. Sprinkle in the salt and mix together well.

Spread the granola mixture out over the parchment, making it a little thinner in the middle and piling it up more at the edges, as that's where it will brown more quickly. Bake for 15 minutes, then stir well and continue to cook, stirring the mixture every 10 minutes until golden and fragrant (35–45 minutes in total, depending on how golden you like it). Stir the coconut flakes into the mixture for the final 5–10 minutes. Once ready, remove from the oven and set aside to cool completely.

When ready to serve, heat a griddle pan or a barbecue over a medium-high heat. Brush the cut sides of the fruit with melted butter, place them cut-side down on the griddle, and cook for 2 minutes until lightly charred. Spoon the yoghurt into bowls, top with a hefty sprinkling of granola and the fruit. Some edible flowers look rather pretty, too.

California Living + Eating

**SERVES: 2
PREP: 10 mins
COOK: 5 mins**

Red onion, smoked fish and cream cheese is a heavenly combination to me: it's oily, salty, sharp and creamy. It's also hard to execute badly, but I do think charring the capers and red onion adds a little extra flourish.

SMOKED FISH TARTINE

—

with charred caper and red onion relish

2 tablespoons nonpareille capers,
   rinsed and drained
½ small red onion, thinly sliced
1 teaspoon sherry vinegar
½ teaspoon soft dark brown sugar
2 large slices of sourdough or rye bread
4 tablespoons labneh (for homemade
   version see page 24) or cream cheese
100 g (3½ oz) smoked salmon, trout
   or halibut
½ lemon, cut into wedges
small handful of chopped
   flat-leaf parsley
freshly ground black pepper

If the capers are wet, pat them dry on a piece of paper towel.

Heat a small frying pan (skillet) or saucepan over a medium-high heat. Add the capers and onion and dry-fry them, tossing or stirring regularly, for about 2 minutes until charred in places. Tip in the vinegar and sugar and stir together; take off the heat and tip into a bowl.

Toast the bread (page 24). Spread the toast with the labneh or cream cheese, arrange the smoked fish over the top and spoon over the caper and red onion relish. Squeeze a little lemon juice over the top, scatter with parsley, grind over some black pepper and serve immediately.

California Living + Eating

California Living + Eating

SERVES: 2
PREP: 5 mins

I tend to find most smoothies too sweet for my taste, so my version has an almost equal balance of fruit and vegetables. If you make it using kiwi fruit, it tends to be a little more savoury and ends up vivid green (as pictured). If you use berries it'll be a little sweeter and a deep purple shade. Freezing the chopped fruit the night before means you won't need any ice cubes. I often use chilled chamomile or jasmine tea instead of water, too.

BREAKFAST SMOOTHIE

50 g (2 oz) kale (or other green
    leaves, such as spinach)
50 g (2 oz) cucumber,
    roughly chopped
handful of mint leaves
1 banana, roughly chopped
1 kiwi, peeled and chopped
    (or 100 g/3½ oz mixed berries)
10 g (⅓ oz) fresh ginger root,
    roughly chopped
handful of ice cubes
250 ml (8½ fl oz/1 cup) cold
    water or herbal tea

Put all the ingredients in a blender (ideally a high-speed one, see page 23) and blend until smooth.

California Living + Eating

For me, the phrase 'the California dream'
conjures up thoughts about the food,
the wine, the outdoor lifestyle, the multi-
culturalism, the freedom and opportunity,
the ocean and the climate.

THE GOLDEN STATE

The phrase actually came into being following the California Gold Rush of 1848. It was a huge turning point in the state's history, and meant that for the following 200 years California was viewed by outsiders as a place of success in the new land.

Before 1848, California was a sparsely populated region, not yet declared an official US state, with the land only recently handed over from Mexico to the US following the Mexican-American War. That changed on 24 January in the town of Coloma, about 80 km (50 miles) from the state capital of Sacramento, when gold flakes were discovered in a stream bed of the American River. Despite attempts by its finders (two men building a saw mill on the river banks) to keep it secret, news spread quickly. Within six months there were 4,000 gold miners in the area. By 1849 over 80,000 people had arrived, and over the following 4 years that number grew to 300,000.

The peak of the gold rush was in 1852, after which the gold deposits were depleted – by the late 1850s most of the mining towns that had quickly come into being were ghost towns. But the long-term effect of the gold rush was dramatic. California was officially made a US state in 1850, investments in infrastructure brought more roads and housing, and the population boomed, with gold-seekers coming from all over North America and as far and wide as Europe, Australia and Asia.

The beginnings of those multicultural communities and the injection into California's economy were crucial. It was firmly placed on the world map and word spread of that 'California dream', drawing more and more people from around the world and making it the unique and culturally rich place it is today. It's also why it's known as the Golden State!

SERVES: 1
PREP: 5 mins
COOK: 10 mins

*At some point, every time I stay in LA, I make this for breakfast.
It's almost as though I forget about smoked turkey until I'm in a US
supermarket – they seem to consume far more of it than we do in the
UK. It's light and lean and makes a nice alternative to smoked salmon.
This is a perfect breakfast for one, either served on thick slices of rye
bread or an onion bagel. Cream cheese can easily replace the mayo, too.*

SMOKED TURKEY BREAKFAST STACKS

California Living + Eating

1 egg
6–8 basil leaves, shredded
1 heaped tablespoon mayonnaise
    (for homemade version see
    page 181)
1 lemon wedge
2 slices of rye bread (or a halved
    bagel), toasted
4 slices (about 80 g/3 oz)
    of smoked turkey
½ avocado, peeled, halved and sliced
1 tomato, sliced
sea salt and freshly ground
    black pepper
handful of mustard cress
    or alfalfa sprouts, to serve

Lower the egg into a pan of boiling water and simmer for 6½ minutes. Drain and cool in cold water.

Mix the basil into the mayonnaise, season lightly with salt and pepper and add a splash of lemon juice. Spread the mayo over the toast and top with the turkey, sliced avocado and tomato. Peel and halve the egg and place on top. Season with salt and pepper and finish with a sprinkling of snipped mustard cress or alfalfa sprouts.

MAKES: 9
PREP: 25 mins +
up to 3 hours rising
and proving
COOK: 30 mins

These vanilla buns are easier to make in a stand mixer with a dough hook, but are perfectly manageable by hand. They're a great breakfast option to feed a crowd on the go.

BREAKFAST BUNS
—

with vanilla and lemon

225 ml (8 fl oz/scant 1 cup) whole (full-fat) milk
125 g (4 oz) unsalted butter, plus extra for greasing
1 teaspoon vanilla bean paste
500 g (1 lb 2 oz/4 cups) strong white bread flour, plus extra for dusting
50 g (2 oz/¼ cup) golden granulated sugar
2 teaspoons easy bake yeast
1 teaspoon fine sea salt
1 egg, lightly beaten
grated zest of 2 lemons

To fill
50 g (2 oz) unsalted butter, softened
100 g (3½ oz/scant ½ cup) golden granulated sugar
1 teaspoon ground cinnamon

To glaze
50 g (2 oz) unsalted butter, melted
1 tablespoon golden granulated sugar

Warm the milk, butter and vanilla in a saucepan until the butter has just melted. Remove from the heat.

Put the flour, sugar, yeast and salt in the bowl of stand mixer fitted with a dough hook and mix. Make a well in the middle and pour in the egg, lemon zest and warm milk-butter mixture. Mix on a slow speed until everything is combined, then increase the speed to medium and knead for 5–6 minutes (or mix everything in a large bowl, then turn out onto a work surface and knead by hand for 10 minutes). Scoop the dough up from the edges so it's not sticking, then put it back in the bowl, cover with cling film (plastic wrap) and leave to rise until doubled in size. This could take 1 hour on a warm day, or up to 2 hours on a cool day (or you can chill it overnight at this stage, letting it come back to room temperature, out of the fridge, before continuing).

When the dough has nearly doubled in size, lightly grease a 23 cm (9 in) square, deep cake tin (pan). For the filling, beat the butter, sugar and cinnamon together with a wooden spoon in a mixing bowl.

On a lightly floured surface, roll the dough out to a 35 × 40 cm (14 × 16 in) rectangle, then trim the edges so they are straight. Spread the butter filling evenly all over the top. Starting from one of the shorter sides, roll up the dough into a tight log. Trim the ends and slice the log into 9 buns (use a lightly floured bread knife to divide it into 3 pieces before cutting each of these pieces into 3). Place in the prepared tin in 3 rows of 3 buns. Cover with cling film and leave to prove at room temperature for 45–50 minutes.

Preheat a fan oven to 160°C (320°F/gas 4). Remove the cling film, brush the buns with melted butter and sprinkle with sugar. Bake for 25–30 minutes until deep golden. Remove from the oven and leave to cool in the pan, then transfer to a rack to cool completely. These are best eaten the day they're made, but can be stored in an airtight container and warmed in a low oven the next day.

SERVES: 2
PREP: 10 mins
COOK: 20 mins

I feel like it would be wrong not to include pancakes in a book of recipes inspired by the States. They are, after all, the iconic American breakfast food. These are made with buttermilk for a fluffy interior.

BUTTERMILK PANCAKES

—

with blueberry cinnamon syrup

150 g (5 oz/1¼ cups) plain
   (all-purpose) flour
50 g (2 oz/¼ cup) golden caster
   (superfine) sugar
¼ teaspoon fine sea salt
1 teaspoon bicarbonate of soda
   (baking soda)
1 egg
100 ml (3½ fl oz/scant ½ cup)
   whole (full-fat) milk
150 ml (5½ fl oz/⅔ cup) buttermilk
50 g (2 oz/¼ cup) unsalted
   butter, melted
4 tablespoons Greek yoghurt, to serve

Blueberry cinnamon syrup
200 g (7 oz) blueberries
3 tablespoons maple syrup
1 small cinnamon stick
¼ teaspoon vanilla bean paste

For the syrup, put half of the blueberries in a small saucepan with the maple syrup, cinnamon and vanilla. Bring to the boil, then turn down to simmer gently for 3–4 minutes until the berries have just burst. Take off the heat, stir in the remaining blueberries and set aside to cool.

For the pancakes, mix the flour, sugar, salt and bicarbonate of soda in a mixing bowl. In a jug whisk together the egg and milk, then stir in the buttermilk and 1 tablespoon of melted butter. Make a well in the middle of the dry ingredients and pour in the buttermilk mixture. Whisk very gently until combined, but don't over-whisk or your pancakes risk being tough. A few lumps are fine (even preferable).

I make 3 medium pancakes per person, about 10 cm (4 in) in diameter, cooking them two at time, but you can vary the size as you like. Heat a large frying pan (skillet) over a medium heat (you may need to adjust the heat once you start cooking). Add a spoonful of melted butter and 2 separate ladlefuls of the pancake batter. After about 3 minutes you should see bubbles appear on the surface. Flip and cook for another 3 minutes. Set aside while you make the rest, adding more butter and batter to the pan. Pile the pancakes onto plates and top with the yoghurt and blueberry cinnamon syrup (discarding the cinnamon stick).

—

NOTES ON… BUTTERMILK
Buttermilk, the dairy by-product of churning cream into butter, is pretty widely available nowadays. It's low in fat (most of the fat solids end up in the butter) and reasonably acidic, so if you can't get hold of buttermilk use natural yoghurt instead, loosened with a little milk and lemon juice. In baking, buttermilk is usually used alongside bicarbonate of soda – a raising agent that is activated by acid – to give a light, airy crumb to cakes and pancakes.

California Living + Eating

I'm a huge fan of savoury breakfasts, because I like to eat at least one (though more often two or three) portions of vegetables to fuel me at the beginning of the day. But sometimes I can be swayed by a pastry. These brioche buns, and the vanilla buns on page 42, aren't too sweet, and are great for an on-the-go breakfast. It is undoubtedly easier to make yeasted doughs in a stand mixer with a dough hook, particularly brioche, as it contains a reasonable amount of butter. If you take on the challenge of making brioche by hand, be patient and accept your hands will get quite buttery, but eventually the fat will incorporate into the dough.

**MAKES: 6
PREP: 30 mins +
up to 4 hours rising
and proving
COOK: 15 mins**

BRIOCHE BUNS
—

with peaches

125 g (4 oz/1 cup) strong white bread
    flour, plus extra for dusting
50 g (2 oz/generous ¼ cup) soft light
    brown sugar
1 teaspoon easy bake yeast
½ teaspoon fine sea salt
2 eggs, beaten
3 tablespoons whole (full-fat) milk
100 g (3½ oz) unsalted butter,
    softened

To top
1 egg yolk, beaten
1–2 tablespoons golden caster
    (superfine) or granulated sugar
2 ripe peaches, halved, stoned
    and sliced

Put the flour, sugar, yeast and salt in the bowl of a stand mixer fitted with a dough hook and mix. Using a fork, beat together the eggs and milk then, with the mixer on a slow speed, pour the mixture into the flour.

Once incorporated, keep the mixer running and add the butter in 4 additions, making sure it's completely incorporated before adding the next bit; keep scraping the dough down from the sides of the bowl with a spatula, if necessary. Knead on a medium speed for 5 minutes. Scrape the dough into a ball and leave in the bowl, covered with cling film (plastic wrap), to rise until doubled in size. This could take 1 hour on a warm day, or up to 2 hours on a cool day (or you can chill it overnight at this stage, letting it come back to room temperature, out of the fridge, before continuing).

Line a large baking tray (pan) with baking parchment. Knock back the dough and divide it into 6 pieces (roughly 90 g/3 oz each). On a lightly floured surface, roll out each piece to form a 10–12 cm (4–5 in) circle. Place on the prepared baking tray. Cover with cling film and leave to prove for about 1 hour, at room temperature, until slightly puffed up.

Preheat a fan oven to 160°C (320°F/gas 4). Brush the tops with the egg yolk, then sprinkle over the sugar. Arrange the sliced peaches on top, then bake for 10–12 minutes, turning the tray halfway if they brown more on one side than the other. Remove from the oven. These are best eaten the day they're made, but can be stored in an airtight container and warmed in a low oven the next day.

SERVES: 2
PREP: 15 mins
COOK: 15 mins

Crab for breakfast seems like a bit of a luxury, but this recipe is fresh, light and zesty and an extremely good way to start the weekend.

CRAB OMELETTE

—

with chilli and sweetcorn

100 g (3½ oz) pre-cooked fresh
   white crab meat
1 lime, grated zest and juice of
   ½ and the rest cut into wedges
1 corn on the cob (or 150 g/5 oz
   frozen or tinned sweetcorn)
3 teaspoons sunflower oil, plus extra
   if needed
10 g (⅓ oz) peeled fresh ginger root,
   thinly sliced then cut into
   matchsticks
1 garlic clove, thinly sliced
1 red chilli, thinly sliced (seeded
   if liked)
½ hispi or pointed spring cabbage,
   core removed and leaves finely
   shredded
4 eggs
1 teaspoon toasted sesame oil
½ avocado, peeled, halved and sliced
sea salt and freshly ground
   black pepper

Mix the crab meat, lime zest and juice in a bowl, season with salt and pepper and set aside.

Slice the corn kernels from the cob by holding the cob upright on a chopping board and using a sharp knife to cut down against the kernels. (I've also seen people do this onto a dish towel, so you can gather up the kernels more easily.)

Heat 2 teaspoons of the sunflower oil in a large frying pan (skillet) or wok over a medium-high heat. Add the corn and a pinch of salt and fry, stirring, for 2–3 minutes then add the ginger, garlic and chilli and fry for another 2 minutes. Tip in the shredded cabbage, season with salt and pepper and stir-fry for another 2–3 minutes until the cabbage is charred in places; squeeze over a little more lime juice and set aside.

Lightly beat the eggs in a bowl with the sesame oil and season with salt and pepper. Heat the remaining sunflower oil in a small non-stick omelette pan or frying pan (skillet) set over a medium heat. Tip in half the egg mixture and fry, swirling the mixture to move the unset egg on top towards the edges, for 2–3 minutes until set. Shuffle the omelette onto a plate and cook the second omelette (adding a splash more oil to the pan, if needed).

Pile the cabbage and corn onto the omelettes, then fold the omelette in half over the filling and top with the crab meat and avocado. Serve immediately, with lime wedges.

AVOCADOS

I grew up eating avocado vinaigrette, though only on special occasions. It was a dinner-party starter that my parents would serve – half an avocado, skin left on but the stone removed and replaced with a punchy Dijon dressing – and while all the adults were seated around the table, I'd have my own bowlful (so it couldn't roll way) to devour in front of the TV. I don't think I ate it any other way until my 20s. And then suddenly a whole new way of eating avocado opened up and I've never looked back.

I think it's safe to say the whole world has gone a little crazy for avocado over the last 20 years. We eat them prepared in all sorts of ways, and at any mealtime. But we're not just talking about any avocado; it's the Hass variety – with the coarse, knobbly skin that creates a protective shield for the buttery flesh – that we all want.

Although avocados are actually a native Central American crop, the original Hass avocado tree was said to be planted in 1926 in La Habra Heights, Los Angeles County, California. The credit goes to Rudolph Hass, a postman who read an article about avocado trees in a magazine, bought some seeds and experimented with growing a few different varieties. He had mixed results, but there was one particular tree that stood out. The fruit grew quicker than on the other trees, its flesh was noticeably more creamy and its crocodile-green skin was thicker and less susceptible to bruising. The tree also grew upright (other varieties were more spread out) making it more feasible to farm. So he started to plant more trees, sold the seeds to some of his co-workers, and eventually patented the 'Hass avocado' in 1935.

That original tree is no longer alive, but now the Hass variety accounts for 90 per cent of Californian (and worldwide) avocado growth and there are groves planted up and down the state's central coast, producing tons of lush fruit every year (though June is peak eating season). So it's quite right that the Californians should be proud of their avocados.

SERVES: 2
PREP: 15 mins
COOK: 35 mins

*A neatly wrapped parcel stuffed with all the greatest breakfast foods
is hard to beat and it's perfect for road trips. There are countless filling
variations – black beans, mole sauce, sliced steak – but I like to keep
it pretty classic and mellow in flavour on the inside and then spoon
over a sharp salsa to cut through it all.*

BREAKFAST BURRITOS
—

with Cheddar scramble, crispy potatoes and coriander salsa

6 slices smoked streaky bacon
    or Millionaire's Bacon (page 58)
1 large waxy potato (such as a
    Charlotte), cut into 1–2 cm
    (½–¾ in) chunks
½ tablespoon olive oil
¼ teaspoon hot smoked paprika
2 tablespoons sour cream
    or Greek yoghurt
1 teaspoon chipotle chilli paste
    or hot sauce (for homemade version
    see page 184)
4 eggs
40 g (1½ oz) smoked Cheddar, grated
10 g (½ oz) unsalted butter
1 tablespoon chopped chives
2 large flour tortilla wraps
½ avocado, peeled, halved and sliced
sea salt and freshly ground
    black pepper

Coriander salsa
25 g (¾ oz) coriander (cilantro),
    chopped
1 tablespoon cider vinegar
½–1 green chilli, roughly chopped
    (seeded if liked)
1 tablespoon water

Preheat a fan oven to 160°C (320°F/gas 4).

Line a large baking tray (pan) with baking parchment and lay the bacon
slices out on one half of the parchment. Toss the chopped potato with the
oil and paprika, season with salt and pepper and arrange on the other half
of the parchment. Roast for 15 minutes, then turn the bacon and toss the
potatoes and roast for another 15 minutes. The bacon should be crisp and
the potatoes golden.

To make the salsa, put all the ingredients in a food processor and blitz to a
rough paste (adding a little more water, if needed), then set aside in a bowl.
In another small bowl, mix the sour cream or yoghurt with the chilli paste;
set aside.

Crack the eggs into a third bowl, beat them, season with salt and pepper and
stir through the grated cheese. Melt the butter in a saucepan over a medium
heat, tip in the eggs and cook, stirring regularly with a spatula, until the eggs
form soft, ripple-y curds. Take off the heat a little before they're done (they'll
continue to cook a bit in the pan) and stir through the chives.

To build the burritos, lay out the wraps on a board. Spread each with the
chipotle sour cream, then spoon the eggs down the middle, topping them with
the bacon, potatoes and avocado. Fold over the top and bottom of the tortilla,
then roll up from one side as tightly as you can. Halve and serve with the
coriander salsa.

There's nothing new about toast and jam, but add a lick of whipped ricotta and it's a whole different story. The contrast in temperatures and textures, plus the salt against the sweet, just work brilliantly. The version served at Sqirl in LA is legendary, though it comes served on brioche which is a little too rich for me. I prefer thick slices of seeded sourdough. You can also replace the jam with fresh or cooked fruit: sliced strawberries, fresh figs or roasted grapes are a winner.

SERVES: 2
PREP: 10 mins
+ cooling
COOK: 10 mins

WHIPPED RICOTTA TOAST

—

with blackberry juniper jam

Blackberry juniper jam
(makes 800–900 ml/27–30 fl oz)
6–8 juniper berries
600 g (1 lb 5 oz) blackberries
500 g (1 lb 2 oz/2¼ cups) jam sugar
   (gelling sugar)
juice of 1 lemon

Whipped ricotta
250 g (9 oz/1 cup) ricotta cheese
1–2 tablespoons whole (full-fat) milk
grated zest of ½ lemon
pinch of sea salt

To serve
4 slices of bread

Put a small plate in the freezer (this is for testing the jam later on).

Put the juniper berries into a medium casserole dish (Dutch oven) or stainless steel saucepan. Crush them in the base of the pan with the back of a fork, then stir in the berries and sugar.

Set the pan over a low heat and stir occasionally until the sugar has dissolved. Add the lemon juice, then bring to a vigorous boil. Bubble for 6–8 minutes, skimming off any scum from the top. Take off the heat and place a teaspoon of the jam on the chilled plate. Leave for a few seconds, then push the edge with your finger: the surface of the jam should wrinkle and the edge should move cleanly from the plate though the jam should still be loose. If it's too soft, return the plate to the freezer and let the jam bubble for 2 more minutes before testing again. Repeat boiling and testing until the jam is ready. (Or, if you find that it has set too firm you can always stir in a little boiling water to loosen it.) Take the pan off the heat and leave to stand for 15 minutes, then ladle into clean, sterilised jars (see page 25 for sterilising method). Seal and store in a cool, dark place for up to 6 months. Once open, store in the refrigerator.

To make the whipped ricotta, tip the ricotta into a mixing bowl. Add 1 tablespoon of milk and use a balloon whisk to whip it up. Whisk in the lemon zest and salt and chill until ready to serve.

When ready to serve, toast the bread, spread it generously with chilled whipped ricotta and spoon over the jam.

Cornbread is a staple of America's southern states, originally made because polenta (cornmeal) was a cheaper alternative to wheat flour. It makes great breakfast food and the addition of maple syrup and bacon here is a total winner. If you don't have an ovenproof frying pan (skillet), you can adapt the method slightly and bake the bread in a 20 cm (8 in) cake tin (pan). This recipe actually makes enough cornbread for 8 people, so you can double up the rest of the ingredients if you want to make this recipe for a crowd (in which case I'd serve it with soft-boiled instead of poached eggs).

SERVES: 4
PREP: 15 mins
COOK: 30 mins

MAPLE BACON CORNBREAD

—

with poached eggs and pickled jalapeño

Pickled jalapeño
1 jalapeño chilli, thinly sliced
1 tablespoon cider vinegar
1 teaspoon maple syrup
pinch of sea salt

Maple bacon cornbread
100 g (3½ oz) smoked streaky bacon
  slices, chopped
150 g (5 oz/1 cup) polenta (cornmeal)
150 g (5 oz/1¼ cups) plain
  (all-purpose) flour
½ teaspoon fine sea salt
½ teaspoon bicarbonate of soda
  (baking soda)
½ teaspoon baking powder
300 ml (10 fl oz/1¼ cups) buttermilk
1 egg, lightly beaten
4 tablespoons maple syrup
100 g (3½ oz) unsalted butter

To serve
4 slices of Monterey Jack or
  Cheddar cheese
4 eggs
2–4 tablespoons hot sauce
  (for homemade version
  see page 184)

Preheat a fan oven to 180°C (380°F/gas 6).

Mix all the pickled jalapeño ingredients together in a bowl and set aside.

To make the cornbread, fry the bacon in an ovenproof frying pan (skillet) (about 20 cm/8 in across the base) over a medium heat for about 5 minutes until golden, then lift it out with a slotted spoon and set aside on paper towels. Set the pan aside, leaving any bacon fat in it.

In a large bowl, mix all the dry ingredients. In a separate jug, beat the buttermilk, egg and 3 tablespoons of the maple syrup, then whisk this wet mixture into the dry ingredients, along with the fried bacon bits. Melt 50 g (2 oz) of the butter and stir it through the cornbread mixture until combined.

Put the pan with the bacon fat back over a medium heat and add 30 g (1 oz) of the butter. As soon as it's foaming, tip in the batter and smooth the surface with the back of a spoon. Transfer the pan to the oven and bake for 20 minutes.

Meanwhile, make a glaze by melting the remaining 20 g (¾ oz) butter and tablespoon of maple syrup together in a pan. Brush this over the top of the cornbread, then return to the oven for another 5 minutes. The cornbread should now be golden and a skewer inserted into the middle should come out clean. Remove from the oven and set aside to cool.

Preheat the grill (broiler) to medium-high (240°C/460°F) and line a baking tray (pan) with kitchen foil. Slice the cornbread (I like to serve one big wedge per person). Arrange on the lined tray and top each cornbread wedge with a slice of cheese.

Poach the eggs in a wide pan of barely simmering water for 3–4 minutes, or until set (see page opposite). Lift out and drain on paper towel while you grill the cornbread.

Pop the cornbread under the grill for a couple of minutes. Top each portion with a drizzle of hot sauce, a poached egg and then sprinkle over the drained pickled jalapeños.

Even with professional training and years of kitchen experience, I sometimes find the idea of cooking eggs to serve more than two people a daunting prospect. Getting them just right requires a little technique and practice and, of course, being aware of your personal preference.

NOTES ON...
COOKING EGGS

FRYING

For any kind of egg frying, a good, heavy non-stick frying pan (skillet) will help. Fried eggs are a personal thing. I like them gently crispy at the edges, but some people prefer them golden and lacy on the bottom and others want a soft white all over, so set the heat under the pan accordingly. Use oil (olive or sunflower) for frying as the milk solids in butter can burn. Once the whites have set beneath, tilt the pan a little so you can scoop up the excess hot oil with a spoon and drizzle it over the yolks to help them cook from above.

SCRAMBLING

In the burrito recipe (page 50) I suggest a slightly firmer scramble than I would if serving scrambled eggs on their own. Usually I stick to the classic French method of scrambling eggs, which is achieved by cooking them at a milder temperature than most people expect. You want soft, silky curds, and the key is stirring constantly over a low and slow heat – it's almost one step on from making a custard. So add seasoned, beaten eggs (no milk or cream, it's not necessary) and a knob of butter to a small, cold, non-stick saucepan. Set over a medium-low heat, season, and stir constantly with a wooden spoon. If it feels too hot or cooks too quickly, then lift the pan from the heat to cool it. It takes a little while, but you end up with perfect soft-set scrambled egg.

BOILING

How one likes their boiled eggs is a personal matter, though my main concern is always that there should be no unset white. Boiling room-temperature eggs for 6 minutes produces a lovely yolk that is set around the edges but still a little runny within. Reduce to 5½ minutes if you want a classic soft-boil, or take up to 7 minutes for something a little firmer to use in salads (like the niçoise on page 87). The perfect hard-boil takes 10 minutes. There are various methods for boiling eggs, but I always lower room-temperature eggs into a pan of simmering water. It allows for more precise cooking than placing eggs in cold water and waiting for them to come to the boil. Once boiled, always refresh eggs in cold water to stop the cooking.

POACHING

Poaching eggs always fills me with a little dread; however much I practice, the results are a bit hit-and-miss. The most important things I've learned are to use the freshest eggs possible, because the whites are more viscous, and I find chilling them beforehand helps too. Crack the egg into a cup as it's easier to then slip them into the water. Also keep your water at a low simmer, just a few bubbles here and there, swirling it gently with a large spoon and only dropping the egg in once the vortex has died down. They usually take 3–4 minutes for the white to set with the yolks remaining soft. Lift the eggs out with a slotted spoon, drain on paper towel, and season before serving.

OMELETTES

If you don't want to set yourself up for a fall use a good non-stick pan, and one the right size for an omelette: mine is about 20 cm (8 in) across the top and 17 cm (7 in) across the base. Warm the pan with a little oil over a medium heat (personally I think an omelette should never be browned, so a firm but gentle heat is key). Tip in the beaten egg and let it set a little, before swirling to move the unset egg on top towards the edges. You can also draw the set edges into the centre with a fork, letting the uncooked egg pour back out into the pan. At culinary school, we were taught to beat in 1 tablespoon of water for every 2 eggs before cooking, as it lightens the omelette. I can't say I'm convinced, but do try it and see for yourself!

California Living + Eating

SERVES: 4
PREP: 20 mins
COOK: 30 mins

A few years ago a brunch spot in San Francisco rose to fame with its millionaire's bacon, a thick-cut strip of bacon slow-cooked in sugar and cayenne. Here's my simplified version. Its sweetness works well with the sweetcorn fritters, which are ramped up with some kimchi. I tend to serve this with a dollop of yoghurt, some hot chilli sauce and sliced avocado, but a soft-boiled or poached egg is also worthy of consideration.

SWEETCORN + KIMCHI FRITTERS

—

with millionaire's bacon

2 corn on the cob (or about 300 g/
    10½ oz frozen or tinned sweetcorn)
3–4 tablespoons sunflower oil
125 g (4oz/1 cup) self-raising
    (self-rising) flour
½ teaspoon fine sea salt
1 egg
100 ml (3½ fl oz/scant ½ cup)
    whole (full-fat) milk
grated zest of ½ lime
2 spring onions (scallions),
    finely chopped
1 small red (bell) pepper, seeded
    and diced
50 g (2 oz) kimchi, roughly chopped
handful of coriander (cilantro), leaves
    and stalks separated, stalks chopped

Millionaire's bacon
8 slices thick-cut streaky bacon
    (smoked or unsmoked)
1½ tablespoons maple syrup
scant ¼ teaspoon cayenne pepper

To serve
1 avocado, peeled, halved, stoned
    and sliced
4 tablespoons Greek yoghurt
hot sauce (for homemade version
    see page 184) or sriracha

Preheat a fan oven to 160 °C (320 °F/gas 4) and line a baking sheet with baking parchment.

To make the millionaire's bacon, space out the bacon slices on the lined baking sheet and brush them with half the maple syrup. Bake for 10 minutes, then turn them, brush with the remaining maple syrup and scatter with the cayenne. Bake for another 10–15 minutes until golden.

Meanwhile, slice the corn from the cob by holding the cobs upright on a chopping board and using a sharp knife to cut down against the kernels. Heat a frying pan (skillet) over a medium heat. Toss the corn kernels in a bowl with 1 tablespoon of the oil, then tip them into the hot pan. Cook for 2–3 minutes, tossing occasionally, until the kernels are just starting to char, then set aside.

Mix together the flour and salt in a bowl. Beat the egg and milk in a jug and pour into the flour, whisking until smooth. Stir in the lime zest, spring onions, red pepper, kimchi and chopped coriander stalks.

Turn the oven down to 110 °C (225 °F/gas ¼). Heat 2 tablespoons of oil in a large frying pan over a medium heat. Add heaped spoonfuls (about 3 tablespoons in total) of the mixture and fry for 2–3 minutes on each side; you should be able to cook 4 fritters at a time. Drain on paper towels, then transfer to a baking sheet and keep warm in the oven while you fry the remaining fritters, adding more oil, if needed.

Serve 2 fritters per person with 2 bacon rashers, some sliced avocado, yoghurt, hot sauce and the coriander leaves.

—

NOTES ON… SOFT HERB STALKS
Coriander stalks have heaps of flavour and can be used just as well as the leaves. Chopped, they can be added to the base of curries, blended into chilli sauces like the Zhoug on page 104, or added to fishcakes. Likewise chopped parsley stalks can be added to the base of soups and stews, or into meatballs and burgers.

SOURDOUGH

I've heard many people say that the wild yeast in the air that rolls in with the San Francisco fog is what makes the city's bread so unique. Whether that's true or not (most say it's an old wives' tale), there's no doubting that San Francisco-style sourdough is world class.

The roots of sourdough, a bread made with natural yeasts and bacteria that encourage the acid in the dough to slowly ferment and the dough to rise, originate in Europe. And although it is said to have first appeared in California during the Gold Rush (pages 36–37) it was only really during the 1980s craft food revolution that it became widely available.

Today, Chad Robertson of Tartine is widely regarded as the hero of San Francisco sourdough. He opened his original bakery in the city's Mission district in 2002 and although it took a while to gather speed, people now regularly queue around the block for his bread.

As is often the way with the pioneers of California cuisine, Robertson studied traditional baking techniques in France, but on returning to the States he didn't feel bound by them. He cared deeply for sourcing the best flour, but his method of high hydration and long fermentation was far from conventional. The resulting bread, and what many now consider to be the benchmark for San Francisco sourdough, is wonderful. The flavour is deep and sour, the dark crust is almost charred and the crumb is so moist it is commonly described as 'custardy'. Robertson has also generously shared all his knowledge on breadmaking, writing three books on the subject, and has become a guru for many amateur sourdough makers worldwide. The method I use to make sourdough is from *Tartine Bread*, and I would highly recommend it to anyone interested in making sourdough.

At Tartine, slices of San Francisco sourdough might be filled with lightly smoked sheeps' cheese and quince jam or topped with steak tartare and cured egg yolk. I understand now why I see sandwiches and tartines (open sandwiches) so often on Californian menus… because their artisan bread is absolutely worth celebrating.

I'm rather partial to the breakfast sandwiches served at Eggslut, which has various locations in LA. They pack all sorts of breakfast-y deliciousness into a brioche bun with plenty of feisty sauce. This is my version. I struggled to decide whether to include fried or scrambled eggs. Scrambled won out, but either is good and a runny yolk in a breakfast sandwich is always a good thing. A slice of cheese and some pickled cucumbers wouldn't be out of place here either! And if you've never had chicken sausage, I urge you to try it. It's very, very good.

SERVES: 4
PREP: 20 mins
COOK: 25 mins

THE ULTIMATE BREAKFAST SANDWICH

1½ tablespoon sunflower oil
1 garlic clove, bashed
150 g (5 oz) baby leaf greens, shredded
squeeze of lemon juice
10 g (⅓ oz) unsalted butter
2 spring onions (scallions), sliced
8 eggs, beaten
4 brioche buns
sea salt and freshly ground
   black pepper

Chicken sausage patties
350 g (12 oz) minced (ground)
   chicken thighs
⅛ teaspoon ground allspice
sea salt and freshly ground
   black pepper

To serve
green chilli aioli (page 183)
hot sauce (for homemade version
   see page 184)

First shape the chicken sausage patties. Mix the minced chicken in a bowl with the allspice and season with pepper and at least ½ a teaspoon of salt. Shape into 4 patties (wet your hands with water if it starts to stick) – they should be as flat as you can make them; set aside.

To fry the greens, heat ½ tablespoon oil in a large frying pan (skillet) over a medium heat. Add the bashed garlic clove, the shredded greens a pinch of salt and stir-fry for 3–4 minutes until softened and starting to char. Add the lemon juice and toss for another 30 seconds; lift out of the pan, discard the garlic clove and set aside.

To cook the chicken sausage patty, add another tablespoon of oil to the frying pan, return to a medium-high heat and fry the chicken patties for 3–4 minutes on each side until golden and cooked through; set aside.

Put a saucepan over a medium heat. Add the butter and spring onions, season with salt and pepper and cook for a couple of minutes. Tip in the eggs and cook, stirring continuously with a spatula until you have soft, ripple-y curds. Take off the heat a little before they're done as they'll continue to cook in the pan.

To assemble, split the brioche buns then spread each base with a good dollop of aioli or mayo. Layer up with the chicken patty, fried greens, scrambled egg, a drizzle of hot sauce, and finish with the bun lids.

———

NOTES ON… CHICKEN SAUSAGE
Chicken sausage patties are something I've not seen much outside of the States, but I'm a huge fan and will happily eat them as part of a breakfast plate or even as a side with a lunchtime salad. Sometimes I add a little grated apple and chopped sage into the mince too, though ground allspice is always there. It's a rich, deep and fragrant spice and, while we tend to associate more with sweet things in Europe, I think it adds real warmth and backbone to meat dishes.

California Living + Eating

SERVES: 2
PREP: 45 mins
+ resting
COOK: 20 mins

Malawach is a gloriously flaky Yemenite bread, layered with butter, and easy enough to make at home. The only place that I have eaten it outside of Israel is at Kismet in Los Angeles where amazing things are done with Middle Eastern flavours. I love the unpretentious simplicity of this breakfast, it is just homely and comforting.

MALAWACH
—

with boiled egg, tomato and tahini

4 eggs
4 tablespoons tahini
2 tablespoons lemon juice
3 large tomatoes
½ small garlic clove, finely grated
za'atar, to sprinkle
sea salt and freshly ground
    black pepper

Malawach bread
300 g (10½ oz/scant 2½ cups)
    plain (all-purpose) flour, plus
    extra for dusting
½ teaspoon caster (superfine) sugar
1 teaspoon fine sea salt
150 ml (5 fl oz/scant ⅔ cup)
    lukewarm water
175 g (6 oz) unsalted butter, melted
    and cooled slightly
sunflower oil, for greasing
flaky sea salt, to sprinkle
¼ teaspoon nigella (black onion)
    seeds

In a mixing bowl, combine the flour, sugar and salt. With a wooden spoon, mix in the water and 100 g (3½ oz) of the melted butter; rest for 5 minutes. Tip the dough onto a lightly floured surface and knead for 5 minutes until smooth. Rest for 20 minutes on the work surface, covered with a sheet of lightly oiled cling film (plastic wrap).

Halve the dough. On a lightly floured surface, roll out one piece as thinly as possible to a 35 × 40 cm (14 × 16 in) rectangle. Brush all over with melted butter, then starting from the long side fold up about 5cm (2 in) from the bottom. Brush the folded bit with butter, then fold over again, brushing as you go, until you have a long strip of folded dough 35 × 5 cm (14 × 2 in). Tie a knot in the middle of the strip, then tie another knot above it and tuck in the ends. Gently shape into a ball and rest under oiled cling film for another 20 minutes. Repeat this process with the remaining piece of dough.

Hard-boil the eggs in a pan of boiling water for 10 minutes. In a bowl, mix the tahini and lemon juice with enough warm water (about 2–3 tablespoons) to make a smooth sauce; season. Using the coarse side of a box grater, grate the tomatoes (as far as you can while protecting your fingers). Sieve the pulp (discard the excess liquid), tip into a bowl, season and stir in the garlic.

Preheat a fan oven as high as it will go and place a baking sheet on the top shelf to heat up. Place one ball of dough on a large sheet of baking parchment. Press it out with your fingers to make a circle, then roll out to a bigger circle about 28 cm (12 in) in diameter. Brush the top with melted butter, sprinkle with a little flaky sea salt and a few nigella seeds. Slide the parchment onto the hot baking sheet and bake for 4–5 minutes until golden. Repeat to make a second malawach. Serve topped with the tahini, grated tomato and sliced hard-boiled egg, sprinkling a little za'atar over the top.

This is not a recipe as such, but a little bit of an introduction to water kefir (as opposed to milk kefir) which I first discovered in California and was instantly hooked.

Kefir (I say kef-fear, in the States they say kee-fer) is a probiotic, fermented drink that is said to be very beneficial to gut health. It is made by fermenting water kefir grains (which are different to milk kefir grains) in sugary water. The bacteria in the grains eat the sugar turning it into more beneficial bacteria, acids, enzymes and B vitamins. I aim to drink about 100 ml (3½ fl oz/scant ½ cup) every morning on rising, though it is powerful stuff and I have known it to make people feel a little queasy the first time they drink it, so start slowly.

WATER KEFIR

Water kefir is widely available to buy in California and comes in various flavours. My favourite spot to drink it is a brilliant little brewery called The Kefiry in Sebastopol, Sonoma which is dedicated to kefir brewing and where the staff have encyclopedic knowledge on the subject.

You can buy grains from various reputable sources online. Once they arrive you can get brewing immediately. Invest in two good-quality 2-litre (70 fl oz/ 8 cup) jars (such as Kilner or Mason) and a sheet of muslin (cheesecloth). Fill the first jar with 200 ml (7 fl oz/scant 1 cup) hot filtered water and 70 g (2½ oz/ generous ⅓ cup) unrefined golden caster (superfine) sugar. Leave for a couple of minutes, then stir to dissolve the sugar. Top up with 800 ml (27 fl oz/3⅓ cups) cold filtered water and check the water is room temperature (leave it to cool if not) then add 3 tablespoons of water kefir grains. Cover the top of the jar with muslin, but don't seal it, and leave in a cool, dark place. After 48–72 hours, taste the water. It's ready when it no longer tastes sweet, or there's just a hint of the sugar left.

Strain the kefir through a sieve (fine-mesh strainer) into a jug (ideally using a non-metallic sieve). You'll notice the grains left in the sieve will have increased in volume. It's normal for them to grow as they eat the sugar but you only ever need 3 tablespoons per batch so just discard any excess. You can start brewing your next lot of kefir with the grains left in the sieve. The basic formula is 3 tablespoons water kefir: 1 litre (34 fl oz/4 cups) water: 70 g (2½ oz/generous ⅓ cup) unrefined sugar, and with that you can keep going and going!

The strained liquid in the jug, however, is ready for its second ferment and now you can add some aromatics too. Tip the liquid into the second, clean 2-litre (70 fl oz/8 cup) jar and add anything from some freshly sliced ginger root to a handful of berries, or a couple of scooped out passion fruit (my preferred flavour). Seal and leave in a cool, dark place for another 48 hours. When you open the jar, it might open with a pop as the kefir inside is now effervescent. Pass it through a sieve again to remove the aromatics, then pour the kefir into a sealable container (like a glass bottle with a flip-top). Chill and drink a little every day, storing it for no more than 2 weeks.

With breakfast out of the way, next arrives a colourful array of light, bright and beautifully presented plates that appeal at any time of the day. Some make the perfect meal on their own, others are best served together on a big sharing table laden with other tasty bits: salted butter, crusty bread, jars of pickled vegetables, even a whole roasted chicken or a side of salmon.

ALL DAY
EVERY DAY

I've never understood why gazpacho isn't on more menus in southern Californian restaurants. It is, in essence, a salad smoothie, light and refreshing and well-suited to the climate. I've substituted white bread, which is traditionally used to create the velvety body of the soup, with cashews. They do the same job and seem more in keeping with the Californian spirit. Go easy with the garlic: grate in a little at a time, tasting as you go, or leave it out entirely and it's still wonderful. This recipe makes about 500 ml (18 fl oz/2¼ cups), which is about right for 2 people, though you can easily double or triple the ingredients to serve more.

SERVES: 2
PREP: 15 mins

CASHEW GAZPACHO

15 whole unsalted cashews
(25 g/¾ oz)
3 tablespoons extra virgin olive oil,
plus extra for drizzling
1 tablespoon sherry vinegar
½ teaspoon fine sea salt
¼ teaspoon golden caster
(superfine) sugar
2–3 medium tomatoes (250 g/9 oz),
roughly chopped
¼ cucumber (100 g/3½ oz),
roughly chopped
½ red (bell) pepper (50 g/2 oz),
seeded and roughly chopped
1 spring onion (scallion),
roughly chopped
¼ garlic clove, finely grated (optional)
75 ml (2½ fl oz/5 tablespoons)
cold water
freshly ground black pepper
edible flowers, to garnish

Soak the cashews in a bowl of cold water while you prepare all the other ingredients.

Put the oil, vinegar, salt and sugar in the jug of a high-speed blender (page 23). Add the tomatoes, cucumber, pepper and spring onion, along with a small grating of garlic.

Drain the cashews and tip them in, then add the cold water and blend.

Stop and scrape down the sides, if needed, and blend again. Check the seasoning and add more salt, sugar, garlic or vinegar to balance; a grind of black pepper is nice too. You may also need to add a splash more water to achieve the desired consistency. Blend again until really smooth. Gazpacho is best served well chilled, so pop it in the refrigerator for an hour before serving in bowls or glasses, garnished with edible flowers and a drizzle of oil. Or serve immediately with a cube of ice in each bowl.

California Living + Eating

The Chinese chicken salad is an archetypally Californian dish. An invention of the 1960s when 'exotic' flavours were all the rage, and original ingredients commonly included (ahem) tinned mandarin segments and crispy wonton strips. There was very little that was actually Chinese about it, but Californian diners were hooked. And its popularity really has endured as you still find evolved versions of it everywhere. This is mine. Sometimes I arrange all the prepared ingredients on a board with some Vietnamese rice paper wrappers and turn them into summer rolls, using the dressing as a dipping sauce. It's a nice way to mix it up, and fun for a dinner party. This recipe is just as good without the chicken, too.

SERVES: 4
PREP: 25 mins
COOK: 10 mins

ASIAN-STYLE CHICKEN SALAD
—
with roasted cashew dressing

100 g (3½ oz) dried vermicelli
   rice noodles
splash of groundnut (peanut) oil
¼ small red cabbage, finely shredded
   with a mandoline (about 150 g/
   5 oz prepared weight)
2 large carrots, shredded with
   a julienne peeler (about 150 g/
   5 oz prepared weight)
2 spring onions (scallions),
   cut into 5 cm (2 in) pieces and
   shredded lengthways
100 g (5 oz) sugar snap peas,
   sliced on the diagonal
1 red chilli, seeded and sliced
1 ripe mango, peeled, cut to make
   2 'cheeks' and sliced into strips
2 cooked chicken breasts, shredded
handful of mint leaves
handful of Thai basil leaves

Roasted cashew dressing
100 g (5 oz/⅔ cup) unsalted cashews
1 tablespoon maple syrup
1½ tablespoons fish sauce
3 tablespoons water
juice of 1 lime

Preheat a fan oven to 160°C (320°F/gas 4).

To make the dressing, put the cashews in a roasting tray (pan) and roast for 5 minutes. Stir through the maple syrup and roast for another 5 minutes until golden. Tip straight onto a piece of baking parchment (they'll stick to the tray otherwise) and cool.

Meanwhile, prepare the vermicelli noodles according to the packet instructions. I usually soak them in a bowl of cold water for 10 minutes, then drain. If they're still a bit hard, cover them with just-boiled water from the kettle. Immediately drain in a sieve (fine-mesh strainer) and rinse under the cold tap, then toss with a splash of groundnut oil to stop them sticking and leave them to dry on a double layer of paper towel.

To finish the dressing, put the fish sauce, lime juice, water and two-thirds of the roasted cashews in a high-speed blender (page 23). Blitz until smooth, adding a splash more water, if needed. Roughly chop the remaining cashews.

Toss the veg, chilli and noodles in a large bowl. Top with the mango and shredded chicken and spoon over the dressing. Scatter with the herbs and the remaining cashews.

—

NOTES ON… COOKING CHICKEN BREASTS
Poaching is a gentle cooking method that is perfect for skinless chicken breasts. When a recipe calls for cooked chicken breast, I usually see it as an excuse to make a big batch of stock (page 24), which also yields two perfectly poached chicken breasts. If cooking breasts from raw, bring a medium saucepan of salted water to the simmer. Slip in the chicken breasts, cover with a lid, take off the heat and leave for 15 minutes, turning them halfway. Lift the chicken out of the water and check they're cooked through. I also like barbecuing and griddling chicken breasts, bashing them out first to an equal thickness between 2 sheets of cling film (plastic wrap) so they cook evenly, which would be great in this salad.

This is based on a recipe I was taught while studying at Matthew Kenney Culinary in LA. I loved how the avocado was unashamedly the star of the show: we often make tomato salads or lettuce salads, but rarely is avocado allowed to sit so boldly on its own despite us eating it with just about anything nowadays. I've been making this dressing for years. I remember the first time I made it, being amazed at how raw carrot can blend into something so creamy. This makes far more dressing than you'll need, so store the leftover dressing in a sealed jar in the refrigerator for up to a week and spoon over all sorts of salads, veg, fish and chicken.

SERVES: 4
PREP: 20 mins

AVOCADO, RADISH + WALNUTS
—
with carrot-miso dressing

100 g (3½ oz) mixed radishes, rinsed
3 avocados, peeled, halved and stoned
30 g (1 oz) toasted walnuts
(see method on page 25)
large handful of chopped coriander
(cilantro) or microherbs (such
as coriander or purple basil)

Carrot-miso dressing
2 tablespoons sunflower oil
1 teaspoon toasted sesame oil
2 tablespoons Japanese rice vinegar
2 tablespoons soy sauce
3 tablespoons white miso paste
1 spring onion (scallion),
roughly chopped
1 small garlic clove, roughly chopped
1 medium carrot, peeled and diced
1 tablespoon grated fresh ginger root
2 teaspoons runny honey

Trim and thinly slice the radishes. If you have time, place them in a bowl of iced water while you prepare the rest of the salad as it will help to crisp them up and give even more of a textural contrast to the avocado.

To make the dressing, place all the ingredients in a high-speed blender (page 23) and blitz until smooth. Check the seasoning: it should be salty and sweet in just the right balance.

Cut the avocado halves into thick slices; I tend to cut them into irregular shapes as the contrasting heights and shapes look quite striking. Arrange over a serving plate. Drizzle with a little dressing.

If you have soaked the radishes, drain and pat dry with paper towels, then scatter them over the avocado. Roughly break up the walnuts and sprinkle over the top, along with the herbs. Spoon over more dressing, serving a little extra on the side.

—

NOTES ON… RADISHES
Pretty and pink, radishes can lift what might otherwise be a dull-looking plate of food. But they offer more than just aesthetics; they have a lovely crispness and a gentle pepperiness that is quite unique in the vegetable world. In California you see watermelon radishes being used a lot (see the Salmon noodle bowls on page 111) They're larger, about the size of a small beetroot, and a little less peppery, but when sliced, their mellow green skin fades to white before revealing a jewelled magenta heart. Do grab a bunch if you see them, and thinly slice them unashamedly over all of your salads!

California Living + Eating

SERVES: 4
PREP: 25 mins
COOK: 1 hr 30 mins

I admit there is nothing new about beetroot (beet) and goat's cheese. It's a combination that we know works. But this is based on a dish I ate with my brilliant photographer Nassima at an inspiring café/foodstore/ market called Shed in Healdsburg, Sonoma. The gentle spicing of the vinaigrette, the sweetness of the stone fruit and the beetroot prepared two ways was just superb, and wholly worthy of replicating.

BEETROOT, GOAT'S CHEESE + STONE FRUIT

—

with spiced vinaigrette

4 purple beetroot (beet), unpeeled
    and trimmed
1 candy striped beetroot (beet),
    unpeeled and trimmed
150 g (5 oz) soft goat's cheese
100 g (3½ oz) Greek yoghurt
grated zest of ½ lemon
1 ripe nectarine, sliced
50 g (2 oz) toasted pecans, chopped
    (see method on page 25)
small handful of tarragon leaves
sea salt and freshly ground
    black pepper

Spiced vinaigrette
½ teaspoon fenugreek seeds
½ teaspoon cumin seeds
½ teaspoon nigella (black onion) seeds
2 cardamom pods, crushed
1 shallot, sliced
1 garlic clove, halved
3 tablespoons groundnut (peanut) oil
1½ tablespoons red wine vinegar

Preheat a fan oven to 140°C (280°F/gas 3).

Rinse the purple beetroot and, with the water still clinging to them, place each on a separate sheet of kitchen foil and loosely scrunch the foil up around it (the residual water helps to steam them). Bake for 1 hour 30 minutes. Check they're cooked by unwrapping the foil and piercing the beetroot with a cutlery knife. If the knife slips in easily, they're ready. Remove from the oven and cool at room temperature (overnight if you like), then unwrap and peel by rubbing off the skin with your fingers, wearing gloves to avoid staining.

To make the vinaigrette, tip the spices into a cold, small saucepan with the shallot, garlic and oil. Set over a low heat and warm very gently, slowly infusing the oil. After 6–8 minutes the onion and garlic should be turning golden and the mixture fragrant. Cool, then drain the oil through a sieve (fine-mesh strainer) into a mixing bowl (I often stir the leftover spices and shallot, discarding the cardamom, through mashed potato). Add the vinegar and season with salt and pepper. Cut the cooked beetroot into wedges and toss them in the vinaigrette.

Peel the candy-striped beetroot, then use a mandoline or a sharp knife to cut it into very thin slices. Mix the goat's cheese in a bowl with the yoghurt and lemon zest. Season with salt and pepper and spread over the base of a serving plate. Lift the purple beetroot from the vinaigrette and arrange over the cheese, along with the sliced nectarine and candy-striped beetroot. Scatter over the pecans and tarragon and drizzle over a little of the vinaigrette to serve.

—

NOTES ON… COOKING BEETROOT
I prefer baking whole beetroot in foil, rather than boiling them, as the flavour is better. You can also roast wedges of beetroot here: scrub (don't peel) whole beetroot, cut into wedges and roast in a little oil in medium oven for 40 minutes. Don't cook candy-striped beetroot as its visual impact is usually lost. If you find eating raw beetroot challenging, massage slices with a little oil and salt and leave for 30 minutes to tenderise.

SALADS:
THE
CALIFORNIAN
WAY

California is often credited with pioneering the 'main-course salad'. When elsewhere salads were seen exclusively as a cold tangle of leaves to accompany a main course, in California the simple addition of protein and some seemingly superfluous extras turned the salad into a bright and bold fully fledged meal in itself.

The beauty of this, of course, is that a salad can be compiled of almost anything. It can comprise countless ingredients, raw or cooked, hot or cold, and can be happily served for lunch or dinner (or even breakfast). So the Californian lesson is to experiment while also paying attention to composition – the colour, the texture, the balance of flavour. I always suggest aiming to have a hint of sweet, sharp, salty and crunch in there too.

SWEET

Californians love fruit in their salads and while, as a Brit, it took me a good while to get my head around the idea, used subtly it can be rather lovely. Try adding thin slices of green apple to salads for a mix of sweet and sharp (page 90), or figs and nectarines for a more honeyed flavour (page 78). Dried fruit like cranberries, raisins or chopped dates are great in slaws.

SHARP

Sharpness often comes from the vinegar or citrus in a dressing, but can come from other ingredients, too. Try adding the shredded peel of preserved lemons (page 25) to a salad, or make quick pickles, left to soak for no more than 30 minutes (page 186) – this is a great way to add bite. As well as veg, think about pickling fruits like plums and cherries – they have a real affinity with mild cheeses.

SALTY

Olives and capers, and cheeses like Parmesan and feta, are quick and obvious salty options, but using cooked salty ingredients, like chunky cubes of crisp pancetta or roasted tamari mushrooms (page 115), also works well and gives salads added texture.

CRUNCH

Toasted nuts and seeds (page 25) are your best friend here, so whenever you're making a batch, go large and store them in airtight containers. I always have roasted cashews, pumpkin and sesame seeds in the cupboard ready to throw over salads. Also, consider firmer veg that can be eaten raw, like shaved or shredded carrot and celeriac, or broccoli stalks and even the florets if they're very small (page 163). Raw, shredded parsnip is also surprisingly good in slaws.

An Angeleno friend claims that the poke craze we've seen sweep the world is actually the Californian appropriation of poke. Originally, poke was a way for Hawaiian fisherman to use the off-cuts or smaller fish from the day's catch, mixing it with whatever they had to hand, usually things like seaweed and maybe soy sauce and onion. Nowadays we are offered infinite toppings, bases, accompaniments and sauces. Whether that is truly down to the Californians I don't know, but this dish is based on my favourite poke bar flavours. You can adapt the toppings according to what you have in the refrigerator: pickled ginger, thinly sliced radish and cucumber, chopped spring onion and steamed broccoli all make regular appearances for me.

SERVES: 2
PREP: 20 mins
COOK: 45 mins

SALMON, CITRUS KALE + BLACK RICE
—

with crispy shallots

100 g (3½ oz) black rice (or about
    200 g/7 oz cooked black rice)
100 g (3½ oz) frozen edamame beans
30 g (1 oz) kale, thick stems removed
    (keep the stems to chop into stews
    or blend into smoothies)
juice of 1 tangerine
2 teaspoons toasted sesame oil
1 tablespoon soy sauce
½ avocado, diced
100 g (3½ oz) raw, sliced
    sushi-grade salmon (see Note
    below)

Crispy shallots
90 ml (3 fl oz/generous ⅓ cup)
    sunflower oil
2 banana shallots, halved
    and quite thinly sliced
pinch of sea salt

Put the rice in a large saucepan and cover with triple the volume of water. Bring to the boil, then turn down the heat and simmer for 40–45 minutes (top up with water if necessary) until tender; drain and spread out on a plate to cool.

In a separate pan of boiling water, simmer the edamame for 3–4 minutes, or until they're all floating on the surface; drain, rinse under the cold tap and set aside.

Meanwhile, tear the kale leaves into bite-sized pieces. Place them in a mixing bowl, add half the tangerine juice and massage the juice into the leaves to soften them. Set aside.

Put the remaining tangerine juice in a jar with the sesame oil and soy sauce. Seal with a lid and shake to make a dressing.

To make the crispy shallots, place the oil and shallots in a cold saucepan, set over a medium-low heat and sprinkle with the salt. The aim is to cook them slowly until they crisp up and turn a medium golden colour, this should take 10–15 minutes. Drain through a sieve (fine-mesh strainer), reserving the oil for dressings and marinades, then transfer the shallots to paper towel to soak up any excess oil.

Toss the cooled rice with the kale and divide between 2 plates. Spoon a little dressing over each. Scatter over the edamame and avocado, then arrange the salmon on top. Spoon over the rest of the dressing, then scatter with crispy shallots to serve.

——

NOTES ON... RAW FISH
It may seem obvious, but if you plan to serve raw fish, then do buy it from a place you know and trust (I go to my local Japanese supermarket), and eat it that day. Of course that's not always possible, so you can replace the raw salmon here with smoked salmon (try thicker-cut tsar fillets), seared tuna, cooked king prawns (shrimp) or fresh white crab meat.

California Living + Eating

Chopped salads are something you see on menus across the States, but less so elsewhere. They are, unsurprisingly, named so because all their ingredients are chopped. They're also completely versatile: as long as you have some leaves, some crunch, some sweetness and some other cooked and raw vegetables it's very much an open canvas. Cheese is usually a must, and I rather like shredded pieces of salami. Dressings too, are open to variation, though oil and vinegar is the perfect speedy option.

SERVES: 2
PREP: 20 mins
COOK: 5 mins

CHOPPED SALAD

100 g (3½ oz) kale, thick stems removed (keep the stems to chop into stews or blend into smoothies)
1 tablespoon extra virgin olive oil
1 tablespoon lemon juice
150 g (5 oz) broad (fava) beans (podded weight)
50 g (2 oz) cos (romaine) or other crisp lettuce, shredded
2 teaspoons balsamic vinegar
handful of chives, finely chopped
50 g (2 oz) semi-hard cheese (I like Morbier), cut into cubes
3–4 slices of finocchiona (fennel salami), cut into strips
½ green apple
sea salt and freshly ground black pepper

Shred the kale leaves, tip them into a large mixing bowl and add the oil and the lemon juice and a pinch of salt. Massage the leaves for a couple of minutes to soften them, then set aside.

Tip the broad beans into a saucepan of boiling water and simmer for 3–4 minutes or until they have all floated to the surface. Drain and rinse under the cold tap. Slip the inner beans from their skins, then toss them into the bowl with the kale. Add the shredded lettuce and vinegar and toss together with a little black pepper.

Fold through the chives, cheese and salami. Thinly slice the apple (this should be done last so it doesn't turn brown) and toss together gently. Serve immediately.

—

NOTES ON... KALE

Although, it feels like kale had its heyday a few years ago now, it still appears in salads everywhere in California, often raw and shredded as here. Varieties of kale vary and some are coarser than others. Strip out the tough stems and shred the leaves – rinse if necessary, then layer up a few leaves on top of each other, roll into a cigar and shred finely with a sharp knife – and massage them with a little acid (lemon juice or vinegar), oil and salt. This should make even the toughest of raw leaves palatable.

California Living + Eating

Soul bowls, grain bowls…whatever you like to call them, these have changed the way we eat lunch (or breakfast, or dinner) in recent years. The key to building a good bowl is in the variety of toppings: some cooked, some raw, different colours, shapes and textures. I usually batch cook all the separate elements in bulk, then assemble different grain bowls through the week. I've also find that roasting quinoa after boiling it is a great way to make it that bit better. It turns nutty and golden, and has much more texture. It's also a genius way of rescuing overcooked quinoa.

**SERVES: 2
PREP: 20 mins
COOK: 1 hr 10 mins**

TOASTED QUINOA BOWLS

—

with roasted almond vinaigrette

25 g (¾ oz/ 2 tablespoons) whole
    skin-on almonds
1 small sweet potato, cut into
    5 mm–1 cm (¼–½ in) rounds
5 tablespoons olive oil
400 g (14 oz) tin of butter (lima)
    beans, drained and rinsed
¼ teaspoon sweet smoked paprika
juice of ½ lemon
100 g (3½ oz/½ cup) quinoa
2 cooked, peeled beetroot (beet),
    cut into wedges (see Note on
    page 78)
100 g (3½ oz) sunflower sprouts
    or pea shoots
sea salt and freshly ground
    black pepper

Pickled red onion
½ small red onion, thinly sliced
1 tablespoon red wine vinegar
1 teaspoon runny honey

Preheat a fan oven to 180°C (350°F/gas 6).

Tip the almonds into a small roasting tray (pan). Toss the sweet potato in a second roasting tray with 1 tablespoon of the oil and season with salt and pepper. Roast the almonds for 6–8 minutes until golden; tip into a bowl to cool. Roast the potatoes for 25–30 minutes, tossing halfway through cooking.

Toss the butter beans in a bowl with 1 tablespoon of the oil, some salt, the paprika and a splash of the lemon juice, then tip into the roasting pan you cooked the almonds in and roast for 12–15 minutes.

Meanwhile, to make the pickle, toss the sliced red onion in a small bowl with the vinegar, honey and a little salt.

Bring a large pan of salted water to the boil, tip in the quinoa and simmer for 12 minutes or until tender but still with a little bite (check pack instructions as cooking times can vary), scooping off any scum that rises to the surface. Drain thoroughly in a sieve (fine-mesh strainer), then spread out on a plate and leave to cool for 10 minutes.

When either the butter beans or sweet potato are cooked, tip into a bowl. Wipe out the tray with paper towel, then tip in the quinoa with another tablespoon of oil and toss; season with salt and another squeeze of lemon juice and roast for 15–20 minutes, stirring halfway, then remove from the oven and set aside to cool slightly.

Lift the onion from its pickling liquid and set aside in a bowl. Add the remaining 2 tablespoons oil to the pickling liquid, then roughly chop the almonds and stir in. Tip into the toasted quinoa and stir together; check the seasoning.

To build the dish, put a layer of the dressed quinoa in the base of a bowl or on a plate. Arrange the butter beans, sweet potato, beetroot and sunflower sprouts over the top. Scatter with the pickled onion, squeeze over any remaining lemon juice and serve.

FARM-TO-TABLE

'The number of ingredients we have access to has multiplied 300-fold since the 1960s,' California chef and food writer Joyce Goldstein told me. 'I shop at the farmers' market (in San Francisco's Ferry Building) every week and I'm always amazed to find something new.'

She credits pioneers of the farm-to-table movement, particularly Chez Panisse's Alice Waters, with changing this. When affordable international travel to and from the US opened up in the 1960s, many young American chefs started travelling in Europe. They were dazzled by the food markets of Mediterranean countries, where in the morning chefs could source the ingredients they wanted to cook that day.

Waters and her peers brought this market tradition back to California. And it became almost a social movement to re-connect people with what they were eating and to care about the land they lived on. They worked closely with farmers and farms, planting all sorts of new crops, changing the dining scene dramatically and proudly name-checking producers on their menus so that their diners could connect what they were eating with where it came from. The Californian climate made it possible to experiment with growing all sorts of non-native plants, the entrepreneurial spirit helped the farming industry to flourish, and today the variety of produce continues to grow and grow.

I've heard many people say the term 'farm-to-table' is overused in Californian restaurants, and I've seen comedians parodying menus that overstate the provenance of their ingredients. But there's no denying California's farm-to-table movement has been hugely influential all over the world. It changed the way we think about what we eat. And, as I mention in my introduction, for the everyday cook the message is very simple: care about your ingredients and where they come from. Your cooking will undeniably taste better for it.

The idea that whatever you're eating – fruit, veg, fish, wine, beer – has arrived at your lips straight from a producer or local supplier is a true California privilege. There are not many places that have this luxury, and there are few places on earth that have that remarkable California geography that incorporates desert, coast, wetlands, mountains, and the numerous microclimates that go along with it. Over 400 crops boldly flourish in California and play a huge part in feeding millions of people across the United States. But 50 years ago, that wasn't the case.

SERVES: 4
PREP: 20 mins
COOK: 20 mins

It's hard to create a bad burrata dish, because burrata in itself is delicious. Simple accompaniments are often best. Here, I like the grassiness of asparagus and the acidity of roasted tomatoes and lemon. The contrast in temperature of the cool cheese and warm tomatoes is rather lovely too. When asparagus is not in season, you can simply leave it out of this recipe, or use another green vegetable, like broccolini.

BURRATA, ASPARAGUS + BLISTERED TOMATOES

California Living + Eating

1 ball burrata (usually 200 g/7 oz)
200 g (7 oz) baby or cherry tomatoes
3 tablespoons extra virgin olive oil
2 garlic cloves, sliced
50 g (2 oz) pitted dry black olives
   (not brined)
¼ small lemon, cut lengthways
   and ends trimmed
1 tablespoon balsamic vinegar
200 g (7 oz) asparagus, trimmed
handful of basil leaves
sea salt and freshly ground
   black pepper
crusty bread, to serve

Preheat a fan oven to 200 °C (400 °F/gas 8). Take the burrata out of the refrigerator at least 30 minutes before you plan to serve it; it shouldn't be eaten fridge-cold.

Toss the tomatoes, oil, garlic and olives in a small roasting tray (pan); everything should fit quite snugly. Thinly slice the lemon and stir into the tray. Season with salt and pepper and roast for 15–18 minutes – you want the tomatoes to blister and the lemon to caramelise. As soon as they come out of the oven, stir in the vinegar.

Meanwhile, simmer the asparagus in a large pan of salted boiling water for 2–3 minutes (thicker spears may need more time, thinner less time). Drain and rinse under the cold tap to stop them cooking further and to retain the colour, then leave to dry on paper towel.

Tear open the burrata and arrange on a serving plate with the asparagus. Spoon over the tomatoes, scatter with the basil and grind over a little black pepper. Serve immediately with crusty bread.

California Living + Eating

SERVES: 2
PREP: 15 mins
COOK: 40 mins

This is the kind of simple dish you can throw together when you don't have much in the house… frozen peas are handy like that.

PEA + BROWN RICE BOWLS
—

with pickled ginger and fried eggs

100 g (3½ oz) brown basmati rice
5 g (¼ oz) peeled fresh ginger
  root, cut into fine matchsticks
1 tablespoon Japanese rice vinegar
2 tablespoons unsalted butter
  or sunflower oil
1 banana shallot, thinly sliced
150 g (5 oz) frozen peas
3 tablespoons water
handful of basil leaves, roughly
  chopped
20 g (¾ oz/¼ cup) toasted flaked
  (slivered) almonds
1 tablespoon sunflower oil
2 eggs
2 lemon wedges
Aleppo pepper (Middle Eastern
  chilli/hot pepper flakes),
  for sprinkling
sea salt and freshly ground
  black pepper

Place the rice in a large saucepan, cover with at least double the amount of water and bring to the boil. Simmer for 25–30 minutes or until tender, then drain.

Meanwhile, mix the ginger in a bowl with the vinegar then set aside.

Rinse out and dry the rice pan and return to a medium heat with the butter or oil. Add the shallot and a pinch of salt and fry gently for 5–6 minutes until softened but not coloured. Tip in the peas and water and simmer for 4–5 minutes until the peas are heated through (it's okay if there's still a little water in the pan).

Tip into a small food processor, season with salt and pepper and blitz until just crushed (you can also use a potato masher or the back of a fork to do this in the pan). Tip into a bowl with the rice and stir together, then check the seasoning and adjust if necessary. Drain the ginger, then stir it through the peas and rice with the basil leaves and almonds.

Heat a small frying pan (skillet) over a medium-high heat and add the oil. Crack in the eggs and fry, tilting the pan a little so the extra fat gathers in the corner and you can scoop it up with a spoon to pour over the yolks. Continue basting the eggs like this as they cook.

Divide the peas and rice between bowls. Top each with an egg, squeeze over a little lemon juice and sprinkle over a little Aleppo pepper.

California Living + Eating

**SERVES: 4
PREP: 20 mins
COOK: 30 mins**

Puy are the king of lentils, tiny slate-grey beads with a firm texture and earthy flavour. They're a good vehicle for salads, but they require an assertive dressing, which they should be tossed in while still hot so they really soak in the flavour.

RED CABBAGE, LENTILS + GOAT'S CHEESE
—
with candied pistachios

125 g (4 oz/⅔ cup) puy lentils
3 tablespoons olive oil
2 tablespoons nonpareille capers,
    drained and rinsed
1 shallot, thinly sliced
1 tablespoon red wine vinegar
200 g (7 oz) red cabbage
handful of chopped flat-leaf parsley
50 g (2 oz) hard goat's cheese
    (such as goat's gouda) or manchego
    or Parmesan, shaved
sea salt and freshly ground
    black pepper
shredded peel of 1–2 preserved
    lemon quarters, to serve, optional
    (for homemade version see
    page 25)

Candied pistachios
½ teaspoon fennel seeds
1 tablespoon caster (superfine) sugar
1 tablespoon water
1 teaspoon unsalted butter
50 g (2 oz/⅓ cup) shelled, unsalted
    pistachios
pinch of sea salt

Put the lentils in a saucepan, cover with cold water and place over a high heat. Once the water comes to the boil, turn down the heat and simmer for about 20 minutes or until the lentils are tender, then drain and tip into a bowl.

Wipe out the pan, add the oil and place over a medium-high heat. Pat the capers dry with kitchen paper, add them to the pan and fry for a couple of minutes, then lower the heat a little, add the shallot and fry for another 3–4 minutes until just softened. Stir in the vinegar, take off the heat and toss the mixture through the warm lentils, season with salt and pepper and set aside.

To make the candied pistachios, toast the fennel seeds in a small, dry frying pan (skillet) for 1 minute until fragrant, then roughly grind in a pestle and mortar. Wipe the pan clean, then add the sugar and water and heat over a low heat. Once the sugar has dissolved, turn up the heat and bubble until syrupy. Stir in the butter and simmer for 1 minute, then add the pistachios, ground fennel seeds and salt. Let it bubble, turning the nuts for 1–2 minutes until they are coated in the syrup, then tip onto baking parchment to cool.

Finely shred the cabbage (use a mandoline if you have one) and toss it through the lentils with the parsley. Tip onto a serving plate and scatter with the candied pistachios and shaved cheese. A little shredded preserved lemon is nice here, too.

—
NOTES ON… FRUIT AND CANDIED NUTS
Boy, do the Californians love fruit in their salads: fresh, dried and often more than one variety. I often throw fine slivers of apple or medjool dates into this salad but, when I'm not in a fruity mood, candied pistachios are a clever way to introduce sweetness as well as a little crunch. This method works with most nuts and you can vary the spices, too, though fennel seeds are undeniably good here.

Zhoug is a Middle Eastern herb and chilli paste that I have rather grown to love and seems to be a very fashionable condiment these days; I've spotted it on many Californian menus recently. For me it has just the right balance of herb, spice and heat, but without the addition of acid that you often find in other sauces of a similar genre – say chimmichurri or salsa verde. Labneh is cool and refreshing, roasted squash is nutty and sweet, and together they make a rather pretty trinity. I often add some toasted pumpkin seeds or quick-pickled sultanas to this salad, too.

SERVES: 4
PREP: 15 mins
COOK: 40 mins

ROASTED SQUASH

—

with labneh and zhoug

1 acorn, onion or kabocha squash,
 halved, ends trimmed, cut into
 2 cm (¾ in) thick wedges and seeds
 scooped out (about 800 g/1 lb 12 oz
 chopped weight)
2 tablespoons olive oil
300 g (10½ oz) Labneh (page 24)
sea salt and freshly ground
 black pepper

Zhoug
1–2 mild green chillies, seeded
 and roughly chopped
1 small garlic clove, roughly chopped
20 g (¾ oz) coriander (cilantro) leaves
10 g (½ oz) flat-leaf parsley leaves
½ teaspoon ground cumin
¼ teaspoon ground coriander
3 tablespoons olive oil
2 tablespoons water

Preheat a fan oven to 180 °C (350 °F/gas 6) and line a flat baking sheet with baking parchment.

Toss the wedges of squash with the oil, then arrange over the lined baking sheet. Season with salt and pepper and roast for 30–40 minutes, turning them halfway, until tender and golden in places.

Meanwhile, make the zhoug. Put all the ingredients in a small food processor and blitz (or finely chop the chillies, garlic and herbs and mix with the spices, oil and water). Add a little more oil or water until you have the consistency of pesto, then season with salt.

Spread the labneh over the base of a large serving plate. Top with the roasted squash and a few spoonfuls of zhoug.

—

NOTES ON… SQUASH
I love the variety of squash that we have available, the different shades, shapes and sizes. I urge you to pick up one you've not used before for this recipe. But do be aware that you can't always eat the skin of the squash. In general, smaller varieties tend to have thinner skins that can be eaten once roasted, and the earlier in the season (which runs from autumn to mid-winter) you're eating them, the more tender they're likely to be. Unless it looks really tough, I usually roast squash with the skin on. The worst case scenario is that it's unpleasant to eat and it needs to be peeled off before serving, which is not all that bad (though it may look a little less attractive on the plate).

California Living + Eating

I'm always slightly frustrated by how hard it is to find sugar- or sweetener-free soft drinks. So I took to making cold-brewed herbal teas a few years ago, and have never looked back. There are hundreds of varieties to play with and these are three of my favourites. I'd always recommend using loose-leaf tea rather than bags, and invest in a good jug with a water infuser for ease. Combine all the ingredients before you go to bed and leave to brew overnight in the refrigerator, then serve over ice with some fresh fruit to garnish. If you don't have an infuser, leave everything in a jug and pass it through a fine sieve the next day.

**MAKES: 1.5 litres
(51 fl oz/6 cups)
PREP: 20 mins**

COLD-BREW HERBAL TEAS

1 tablespoon dried lemon balm leaves
1.5 litres (50 fl oz/6¼ cups)
　　cold water
½ lemon, thinly sliced, plus extra
　　to serve

Lemon balm and lemon
I was put onto lemon balm (also known as Melissa) by a friend who could not stop extolling its virtues: its calming effects, and ability to aid digestion and encourage a restful sleep. It has a subtle but quite 'black tea-like' flavour and is a member of the mint family. If you can ever get your hands on fresh lemon balm, it makes a lovely hot brew.

10 g (½ oz) dried hibiscus flowers
10 strawberry tops
1.5 litres (50 fl oz/6 ¼ cups)
　　cold water
lime wedges, to serve

Hibiscus and strawberry
Hibiscus iced tea, or agua de Jamaica, is a very common Mexican drink. Hibiscus flowers have a slightly sour berry flavour, a little like cranberry, and are simmered in water to produce a concentrate and then sweetened with sugar. This is a simpler version, also using the cut-off green tops of strawberries that might otherwise be discarded.

1 tablespoon dried jasmine green tea
1.5 litres (50 fl oz/6 ¼ cups)
　　cold water
½ green apple, thinly sliced,
　　plus extra to serve

Jasmine and green apple
I have a wonderful mix of jasmine and green tea that I use for this. I can find jasmine a little overpowering when brewed in hot water, but cold brewing gives a more mellow finish that's cut through with green apple.

As daylight fades and the cooler evening breeze sets in, we yearn for richer, heartier and warmer flavours. Turn to elegant entertaining dishes that are perfect for sharing with family and friends.

TWILIGHT

California Living + Eating

I make this kind of dish at least once a week. Once you get used to assembling all the separate components, it's something that can be thrown together very quickly. It is also adaptable to whatever leftover vegetables you have lingering in the refrigerator: often I'll pickle carrot or cucumber instead of radish and add a pile of steamed broccoli or edamame. The chilli-yuzu relish (also known as yuzu kosho), is not strictly necessary, but it does add a lovely extra flourish that I think is worth the trouble. This recipe serves two, but you can easily scale it up to serve more.

**SERVES: 2
PREP: 25 mins
COOK: 15 mins**

SALMON NOODLE BOWLS

—

with chilli relish and pickled radish

125 g (4 oz) dried fine egg noodles
2 teaspoons toasted sesame oil
2 salmon fillets, skin removed
½ tablespoon soy sauce
1 avocado, peeled, halved and stoned
1 teaspoon black sesame seeds
1 spring onion (scallion),
    finely shredded

Quick pickled radish
2 tablespoons Japanese rice vinegar
2 teaspoons runny honey
150 g (5 oz) watermelon radish,
    peeled and thinly sliced

Soy dressing
2 tablespoons soy sauce
1 tablespoon Japanese rice vinegar
1 teaspoon runny honey
1 teaspoon grated fresh ginger root

Chilli-yuzu relish
1 large or 2 small jalapeños
    (or any green chilli), seeded
    and finely chopped
pinch of flaky sea salt
¼ teaspoon concentrated yuzu juice
    (or mandarin or lime juice)
pinch of caster (superfine) sugar
    (optional)

Toss all the pickled radish ingredients in a bowl. Set aside while you prepare everything else, but keep tossing from time to time to coat.

To make the soy dressing, mix all the ingredients together in a bow. Set aside.

To make the chilli-yuzu relish, place the chopped chilli on a chopping board. Sprinkle with a little flaky sea salt and, using the flat side of the blade of a chef's knife, crush the salt into the chilli using a rolling motion. You may need to scrape it up into a pile every now and then, and chop it with the blade to help break down the skin. (Alternatively, pound it in a pestle and mortar or blitz in a small food processor.) Transfer the relish to a bowl and mix in the yuzu juice, and sweeten it with the sugar if required.

Bring a large saucepan of salted water to the boil and drop in the egg noodles, simmer for 3 minutes (or according to the packet instructions), then drain and rinse under the cold tap. Shake to drain, then toss with the sesame oil. Spread out on paper towel to soak up any more excess water.

Preheat the grill (broiler) to medium-high (240 °C/460 °F) and line a baking sheet with kitchen foil. Place the salmon fillets on the lined tray, brush the tops with the soy sauce and grill for 7–8 minutes, or until cooked through.

Divide the noodles between 2 bowls, and spoon over a little soy dressing. Arrange half an avocado and a good heap of pickled radish on each. Place a salmon fillet on each and top with the chilli-yuzu relish. Spoon over the remaining dressing and scatter with sesame seeds and spring onion to serve.

——

NOTES ON… YUZU
Yuzu is a Japanese citrus fruit, with a flavour somewhere between a mandarin and a lime. They're not easy to find fresh, but in Asian (and most large) supermarkets you can often find it sold concentrated in bottles. It really lifts the chilli relish in this recipe, though you can use a splash of lime or mandarin juice instead. Splash leftover yuzu into gin and tonics or chicken noodle soups.

California Living + Eating

San Francisco's Zuni Café, famed for its roast chicken with bread salad, partly inspired this recipe. What also inspired it is a childhood memory of Friday night dinners, the highlight of which was mopping up the gravy straight from the pan with slabs of challah (Jewish bread enriched with oil and eggs). Chunks of bread soaked in golden chicken fat and cooking juices is hard to beat. Using a robust loaf like San Francisco sourdough (preferably one that's a day old) ensures the bread is soft in places but chewy and caramelised in others. Since you end up with less gravy than usual, serve with well-dressed greens or the Courgette, Lemon and Parmesan Salad (page 176) and a bowl of fresh mayonnaise or aioli (page 183).

SERVES: 4
PREP: 15 mins
COOK: 1 hr 10 mins

ROAST CHICKEN
—

with grapes, onions and sourdough

1 medium chicken (about 1.5 kg/
     3 lb 5 oz)
2 onions, sliced
2 garlic cloves, sliced
¼ lemon, thinly sliced
50 ml (2 fl oz/3 tablespoons)
     white wine
50 ml (2 fl oz/3 tablespoons) water
1 loaf of day-old San Francisco
     sourdough, crusts removed and
     torn into chunks (about 250 g/
     9 oz prepared weight)
200 g (7 oz) seedless black grapes
1 sprig of rosemary
sea salt and freshly ground
     black pepper

Preheat a fan oven to 190 °C (375 °F/gas mark 7). Remove any string from the chicken. Trim off the wing and leg tips and excess fat, and toss them in a roasting tray (pan) with the onions, garlic and lemon; season with salt and pepper and pile them up in the middle of the tray.

Season the cavity and the underside of the chicken with salt and pepper, then sit it breast-side down on top of the pile of onions and chicken trimmings, pushing the onions, lemon and garlic underneath as much as possible so they don't burn. Roast for 20 minutes.

Take the roasting tray out of the oven. Using tongs or a long-handled spoon and a fork, lift up the chicken and let any juices pour out of the cavity into the pan. Sit the chicken on a plate and stir the wine into the tray, mixing it through the onions. Spread the onions out over the base, and sit the chicken back in the tray, breast-side up. Season the top of the bird and roast for another 20 minutes.

Take the roasting tray out of the oven and again lift the chicken, letting any juices run into the pan, then sit it on a plate. Stir the water into the tray, then stir in the chunks of sourdough, the grapes and rosemary. Spread everything around the edges of the tray and sit the chicken in the middle. Roast for another 20 minutes.

Lift the chicken out onto a plate (check the juices near the thickest part of the leg run clear) to rest. If the bread isn't golden enough in places, then stir up the onions and bread (remove the leg and wing tips at this stage) and return to the oven for a final 5–10 minutes until golden and sticky.

Carve the chicken and arrange on a large serving plate with the bread, grapes and onions, pouring over any carving and roasting juices.

California Living + Eating

Pictured: Roast Chicken (recipe opposite); Courgette, Lemon and Parmesan Salad (page 176)

This was the centerpiece of my final project while studying at Matthew Kenney Culinary. I spent a week developing the recipe and amazed myself with the intensity of flavour and richness in texture of a raw vegan dish. There are various elements that need to be prepared before assembling the final dish, though none of them is terribly complicated. Such is the way with this kind of food; it requires technique, time and patience to build all the flavours. At Matthew Kenney Culinary we were lucky to work with all sorts of brilliant equipment like dehydrators and vacuum-sealers, but I've adapted this so it can be made in any kitchen, though it no longer qualifies as raw.

SERVES: 2
PREP: 1 hr
COOK: 4 hrs

CORIANDER, COCONUT + DAIKON NOODLE SOUP

Coriander and coconut broth
2 shallots, quartered
2 celery stalks, halved
50 g (2 oz) fresh ginger root, sliced
6 white peppercorns
½ teaspoon coriander seeds
½ teaspoon cumin seeds
pinch of chilli (hot pepper) flakes
2 lemongrass stalks
8 lime leaves
2 garlic cloves, halved
2 litres (70 fl oz/8 cups) water
100 g (3½ oz/generous cup) desiccated
    (dried shredded) coconut
2–3 tablespoons tamari
1–2 teaspoons maple syrup
juice of ½–1 lime
30 g (1 oz) coriander (cilantro)

Sweet potato crisps
1 small sweet potato, peeled
1 tablespoon sunflower oil
1 shallot, thinly sliced

Tamari maple mushrooms
200 g (7 oz) fresh shiitake mushrooms
2 tablespoons tamari
1 tablespoon maple syrup
1 teaspoon toasted sesame oil

To serve
1 daikon, peeled
handful of coriander (cilantro)
    and Thai basil leaves
2 lime wedges

Preheat a fan oven to 130°C (265°F/gas 2).

For the broth, put the shallot, celery, ginger, spices, lemongrass, lime leaves and garlic in a large casserole dish (Dutch oven) with the water. Cover and bake for 3 hours. Remove the casserole from the oven, uncover and cool completely. Pass the broth through a sieve (fine-mesh strainer) into a jug, discarding the aromatics – you should have just over 1 litre (34 fl oz/4 cups). This can be done a day in advance, storing the broth in the refrigerator, then bringing it back to room temperature when needed.

For the sweet potato crisps, use a vegetable peeler to pare long strips from the potato. Toss the strips with the oil and shallot and scatter in a roasting tray (pan).

To make the tamari maple mushrooms, trim the shiitake stems, and halve any larger mushrooms. Toss in a small roasting tray with the tamari, maple syrup and sesame oil. Put the mushrooms and sweet potato in the oven. Roast for 30–40 minutes, turning both every 15 minutes, or until the sweet potato is crisp and the mushrooms have absorbed all the liquid.

Pour the broth into a high-speed blender (see page 23) with the coconut and blitz until smooth. Add the tamari, maple syrup, lime and coriander and blitz again until as smooth as possible, then taste: add more sour (lime), sweet (maple syrup) and salt (tamari) to balance the flavour. Line a sieve with muslin (or paper towel) and set it over a large jug. Pour the broth through the sieve, pressing or squeezing to extract as much liquid as possible.

Spiralize or shred the daikon and place it in a large bowl of iced water for 5 minutes to crisp up. Gather all your other ingredients ready to build the bowls.

Lift out the daikon, then pat it with kitchen towel to absorb as much water as possible. Divide the between 2 large, shallow bowls. Slowly pour the broth (give it a stir if it has separated) around the daikon into the base of the bowls. Arrange the mushrooms, sweet potato and shallot crisps over the top, scatter with the herbs, and finish each with a lime wedge.

I love the beautiful simplicity of this vegetarian supper: a wilting pile of gently poached tomatoes and a cloudy whip of Parmesan-heavy ricotta. Their flavours are harmonious. Eat them with bread (try the Charred Sourdough on page 24), couscous or farro, tossed through pasta, or alongside other salads as part of a big sharing table. Store any leftover tomatoes and oil in a sealed jar in the refrigerator for up to two weeks, using any excess oil in salad dressings.

**SERVES: 4
PREP: 20 mins
COOK:
2 hrs 30 mins**

POACHED TOMATOES

—

with Parmesan and basil ricotta

1 kg (2 lb 4 oz) tomatoes (use a
   variety of colours, sizes and shapes)
5 garlic cloves, halved
3 sprigs of oregano
3 sprigs of thyme
100 ml (3½ fl oz/scant ½ cup)
   extra virgin olive oil
100 ml (3½ fl oz/scant ½ cup)
   light olive oil
sea salt and freshly ground
   black pepper

Parmesan and basil ricotta
350 g (12 oz/scant 1½ cups)
   ricotta cheese
25 g (¾ oz) Parmesan, finely grated
grated zest of ¼ lemon
10 basil leaves, finely shredded,
   plus extra leaves to serve

Preheat a fan oven to 110°C (230°F/gas ½).

Cut any larger tomatoes into 1 cm (½ in) thick slices and halve any smaller tomatoes, then arrange them in a large ovenproof dish. Scatter over the garlic and herbs. Pour over the oil; it won't cover the tomatoes at this stage but it will do by the time they're done. Season with salt and pepper and roast for 2 hours 30 minutes. Remove from the oven (the tomatoes can be cooled and stored at this stage).

Beat all the ricotta ingredients together in a bowl, season with salt and pepper and chill until ready to serve.

California Living + Eating

SERVES: 4
PREP: 25 mins
COOK: 20 mins

This is a wonderful dish of vaguely Vietnamese origins, where it is more commonly served with dill than coriander (cilantro). Both work well in my opinion, or use a mixture of the two herbs.

TURMERIC WHITE FISH

—

with peanuts and chilli-lime cucumber

1½ tablespoons fish sauce
2 teaspoons grated fresh ginger root
2 teaspoons soft light brown sugar
½ tablespoon ground turmeric
4 × 125 g (4 oz) fresh fillets of hake,
    cod or monkfish
2 tablespoons groundnut (peanut) oil
2 large banana shallots, sliced
2 garlic cloves, crushed
sea salt and freshly ground
    black pepper

Chilli-lime cucumber
2 tablespoons lime juice
1½ tablespoons soft light brown sugar
2 tablespoons fish sauce
1 small red chilli, sliced
½ garlic clove, finely grated
150 g (5 oz) cucumber, peeled (if you
    prefer), and thinly sliced
2 tablespoons cold water

To serve
large handful of coriander (cilantro),
    roughly chopped
30 g (1 oz) toasted peanuts (see method
    on page 25), roughly chopped
cooked rice or rice noodles
lime wedges

In a large mixing bowl, mix together the fish sauce, ginger, sugar and turmeric with a good grind of black pepper. Add the fish fillets and turn to coat them in the marinade, then set aside.

In a separate bowl, combine all the chilli-lime cucumber ingredients. Set aside.

Heat a large non-stick sauté or frying pan (skillet) over a medium heat. Add 1 tablespoon of the oil, the shallots and a small pinch of salt. Cook for 3–4 minutes until the shallots start to soften, then add the garlic. Fry for another 3–4 minutes. Scrape out of the pan into a bowl and set aside.

Return the pan to a medium heat with the remaining oil. Add the fish and fry for 3 minutes on each side. Return the shallots and garlic to the pan and add a spoonful of the chilli-lime liquor from the cucumber.

Lift the cucumber from the chilli-lime dressing and divide it among plates, topping it with the fish and shallots. Scatter with the coriander and chopped toasted peanuts and spoon over a little more of the chilli-lime liquor. Serve with rice or rice noodles and lime wedges, and the remaining chilli-lime dressing for spooning over.

California Living + Eating

TACOS

Over the last 10 years the world seems to have gone crazy for tacos. I get it. It's a cheap, relaxed and easy way to eat and it's part of a general global shift in how we eat out, moving away from fine dining and towards more casual set-ups.

'Tacos are something you eat when you have the sand between your toes,' chef Trey Foshee of San Diego's Galaxy Taco told me. It's certainly true in San Diego, southern California's laid-back coastal city that sits on the border with Tijuana in Baja California, Mexico. You go to San Diego for the Baja fish tacos. But in other parts of California you'll find all sorts of other tacos. Tour the street-side stands and trucks in Los Angeles, and you can try pretty much every regional variation going.

Taquerias were originally set up as a quick and inexpensive way to feed Mexican workers. And as Mexico is a huge country with a vast array of culinary styles, the tacos naturally vary from region to region – some use corn tortillas, some wheat, there are different spices, and fillings can range from beef tongue to battered fish, to pork marinated in pineapple. (And to be clear, the corn or wheat shell is the 'tortilla', but when it is filled it becomes a 'taco'.)

The Mexican influence in California is huge. Hispanics are the state's largest ethnic group so it's no surprise that its cuisine is well represented and often brilliantly executed. But tacos are no longer restricted to traditional fillings. In Los Angeles, a city throbbing with strong Mexican and Asian food influences, perhaps it was no surprise that the Kogi BBQ Taco Truck (page 125) became a huge phenomenon, merging Mexican and Korean culinary traditions. It opened the floodgates to a whole new world of cross-cultural variation and experimentation, and nowadays there's a raft of interesting taco options out there. I suppose the reality is that as long as the filling tastes good, it'll probably also taste good wrapped in a tortilla.

I have written three simple taco recipes for this book, inspired by some of the many tacos I've eaten in California – from traditional street-side stands and taco trucks with queues round the block in LA, to beach-front Baja fish tacos and more modern interpretations (including great veggie and vegan versions) at Mexican restaurants up and down the state. I also keep a pack of corn tortillas in my fridge and will happily stuff them with whatever I have to hand. With a little soured cream, pickled red onion and sliced avocado you can pretty much guarantee they'll be good.

The story of LA's Kogi BBQ Taco Truck exemplifies so many things that are trailblazing about the city's food scene. In 2008, Roy Choi, a chef who was born in Korea but raised in LA, started selling his Korean-Mexican hybrid taco in a food truck, building up a colossal following via social media. Kogi was a food phenomenon, paving the way for the food trucks we started to see popping up worldwide and quite dramatically changing the way we eat out. When I tried my first Kogi taco, I was surprised at how simple it was: just some fantastic meat and a simple slaw. So I've kept this recipe pretty straightforward too. I don't even bother with the chilli mayo when I eat them, but I know it's popular with my guests.

SERVES: 4
PREP: 25 mins +
marinating time
COOK: 10 mins

SHORT-RIB TACOS

—

with simple slaw

500 g (1 lb 2 oz) short-rib meat,
   cut off the bone (from about 1 kg/
   2 lb 4 oz short-rib on the bone)
8 corn tortillas, toasted (see method
   on page 128)
lime wedges, to serve

Korean-style chilli bean marinade
2 tablespoons soy sauce
2 tablespoons chilli bean sauce
2 tablespoons Shaoxing rice wine
2 tablespoons soft dark brown sugar
2 garlic cloves, crushed
2 teaspoons grated fresh ginger root
¼ teaspoon ground black pepper

Simple slaw
200 g (7 oz) white or green cabbage,
   finely shredded
1½ tablespoons mirin
juice of 1 lime
handful of roughly chopped
   coriander (cilantro)

Chilli mayo
1 tablespoon chilli sauce (any will do –
   gochujang, sriracha, or the
   homemade version on page 184)
2 tablespoons mayonnaise
   (for homemade version see
   page 183)

If the short-rib meat is on the bone, cut it off in one piece and trim off any silvery sinew or big chunks of fat. Cut each piece of short rib against the grain (as though you're cutting a cross-section of the bone widthways if the bone was still there) into 1 cm (½ in) thick slices.

For the marinade, mix all the ingredients in a large resealable food bag. Add the meat, massage the marinade into the meat through the bag, then chill for at least 1 hour or up to 24 hours.

Preheat the grill (broiler) to high (240°C/460°F) and line a large baking tray (pan) with a double layer of kitchen foil, turning it up at the edges so the juices don't run out. Lift the slices of short-rib meat from the marinade and space them out on the foil; discard the excess marinade. Grill the meat for 5 minutes, then turn it with a pair of tongs, and grill for another 5 minutes on the other side. It should be nicely caramelised in spots and there should be plenty of juices on the foil. Set aside to rest for 5 minutes.

While the beef is cooking, make the slaw and chilli mayo. Toss all the ingredients for the slaw and place in a bowl. Mix the mayo ingredients together in a bowl.

Chop up the rested meat into 1 cm (½ in) cubes and toss with any resting juices. Serve in toasted corn tortillas with the slaw and chilli mayo, and extra lime wedges on the side.

California Living + Eating

Pictured: Baja Fish Tacos (recipe opposite); Cauliflower Tacos (page 128)

SERVES: 4
PREP: 30 mins
COOK: 10 mins

Baja California is a state of Mexico, sitting on the peninsula that stretches down from San Diego through the Pacific Ocean. It is said to be the birthplace of the fish taco, where traditionally the fish is battered and served with a creamy sauce (crema) and pico de gallo (a red, white and green salsa said to evoke the Mexican flag).

BAJA FISH TACOS

—

with lime and cumin crema and avocado pico de gallo

400 g (14 oz) fresh hake or other
   firm white fish
100 g (3½ oz/generous ¾ cup)
   plain (all-purpose) flour
¼ teaspoon cayenne pepper
¼ teaspoon ground cumin
½ teaspoon bicarbonate of soda
   (baking soda)
½ teaspoon fine sea salt
200 ml (7 fl oz/scant 1 cup) beer
   or sparkling water
about 250 ml (8½ fl oz/1 cup)
   sunflower oil, for frying
8 corn tortillas, toasted (for method
   see page 128)
sea salt and freshly ground
   black pepper

Lime and cumin crema
3 tablespoons mayonnaise
   (for homemade version
   see page 183)
3 tablespoons natural yoghurt
¼ teaspoon ground cumin
grated zest of ½ lime and a squeeze
   of juice

Avocado pico de gallo
2 tomatoes, halved widthways
   and seeds discarded
1 avocado, peeled, halved, and diced
1 green chilli, seeded and diced
½ small sweet white onion, diced
juice of ½–1 lime
handful of coriander (cilantro),
   roughly chopped

Start by making the accompaniments. Mix together the ingredients for the lime and cumin crema in a bowl, season with salt and chill until ready to serve. For the pico de gallo, finely dice the tomato halves and toss with the avocado, chilli, onion and lime juice in a bowl; season with salt and chill until ready to serve, stirring through the coriander at the last minute.

Cut the fish into 8 pieces, roughly 2 x 6 cm (¾–2½ in) (don't worry about them being too even). For the batter, combine all the dry ingredients in a mixing bowl. Lightly whisk in the beer (or sparkling water) until just combined – it doesn't matter if it's not completely smooth.

Heat the oil in a large, non-stick sauté pan to about 200°C (400°F). Bear in mind that the temperature will drop as you add the fish so you may need to adjust the heat a little when you start frying. Line a large plate with a double layer of paper towel, and make sure you have a slotted spoon or some tongs to hand.

Dredge the fish, 2–3 pieces at a time, in the batter, then drop into the hot oil (you need to cook them in batches or you'll overcrowd the pan). Cook for about 2 minutes on one side until golden, then carefully turn and cook on the other side for another 2 minutes (you may need to give them a gentle nudge with a spatula if they've stuck to the base of the pan).

Lift out and drain the fish on the paper towel-lined plate, sprinkle with a little salt, then serve on toasted corn tortillas with the pico de gallo and lime and cumin crema.

—

NOTES ON… SHALLOW FRYING
You could use a deep-fat fryer here, but I prefer shallow frying. Use a large, wide, non-stick pan and make sure the oil is really hot before you start. Measure the temperature (200°C/400°F) using a sugar thermometer, or drop a small piece of bread into the pan (it should sizzle immediately and turn golden in 20 seconds). Be careful, keep the your workspace clear, and always take the pan off the heat if it gets too hot.

I really enjoy pulling up at a traditional roadside taco stand where the meaty fillings are as unpretentious as they are delicious, but I've also eaten at plenty of taco places in California where the fillings are thoroughly modern and thrillingly creative. I know nowadays we're all a bit obsessed with roasting cauliflower, but this method of steaming it, then sautéing it in a large pan, gives the cauliflower a really good texture, not too soft but nicely charred in places. I think frying in butter really adds to the flavour, but you can use oil to make this recipe vegan. The creamy cashew sauce here is great too, and can be spooned over just about any vegetables. (See recipe picture on page 126.)

SERVES: 4
PREP: 20 mins
COOK: 15 mins

CAULIFLOWER TACOS

—

with sprout slaw and coriander cashew sauce

1 cauliflower, broken into small florets and core removed (about 600 g/ 1 lb 5 oz prepared weight)
4 tablespoons water
30 g (1 oz) unsalted butter (or sunflower oil)
1 garlic clove, crushed
1 medjool date, pitted and finely chopped (it may be easiest to snip it with clean scissors)
½ teaspoon ground coriander
pinch of ground turmeric
8 corn tortillas
sea salt and freshly ground black pepper

Sprout slaw
100 g (3½ oz) brussels sprouts, trimmed
juice of ½ lime
pinch of sea salt

Herbed cashew dressing
50 g (2 oz/⅓ cup) unsalted cashews
handful of coriander (cilantro)
10 mint leaves
1 teaspoon grated fresh ginger root
1 green chilli, roughly chopped
75 ml (2 ½ fl oz/5 tablespoons) water
pinch of sea salt
½ lime

Soak the cashews in a bowl of cold water.

Put the cauliflower florets in a large sauté pan or shallow casserole dish (Dutch oven) with a lid and add the water. Season with salt and pepper, cover and set over a medium heat. Cook for 5 minutes, shaking from time to time to turn the florets. Remove the lid and add the butter (or oil), garlic and chopped date and toss together with a pinch of salt. Turn the heat up a little and fry for 2–3 minutes, stirring regularly. Tip in the spices and fry, stirring, for another 5–7 minutes until the cauliflower is tender and golden in places. Set aside.

Meanwhile, to make the slaw, finely shred the sprouts and toss them in a bowl with the lime juice and salt.

To make the dressing, drain the cashews then put them in a blender (ideally a high-speed one, see page 23) with the herbs, ginger, chilli, water, salt and a squeeze of lime juice. Blitz until smooth, check the seasoning (adding more lime and a splash more water to loosen, if necessary) then transfer to a bowl.

Toast the tortillas (see Note below), and pile in the cauliflower and sprouts, drizzling with the cashew dressing to serve.

—

NOTES ON... CORN TORTILLAS
It's not always easy to buy pure corn tortillas outside of California, whereas they're ten-a-penny in Californian supermarkets. Their flavour is distinctively corny and their texture more chewy and substantial. Plus, they're smaller than flour tortillas, and each taco here is only meant to be 2–3 bites. There are Mexican (and non-Mexican) supermarkets online you can order them from and I would advise it. I usually buy a variety of 15 cm (6 in) blue and yellow corn tortillas.

I prefer to heat them by lowering them straight onto a naked flame on a low hob and letting them char for about 30 seconds on each side. You can also toast them in a similar way in a dry frying pan (skillet), wrapping the heated tortillas in kitchen foil to keep them warm as you heat the rest.

SERVES: 4
PREP: 30 mins
COOK: 50 mins

I grew up thinking that meatballs belonged on pasta, but I'm not that way inclined any more. Now I believe they should be big and juicy, soaked in a rich tomato sauce and then cloaked in a fine layer of bubbling cheese, served straight from the oven in the pan with a hunk of crusty bread and a green salad to eat alongside, such as the Cavolo Nero and Fennel Salad (see page 172).

PORK MEATBALLS
—
with bubbling cheese and roasted passata

500 g (1lb 2 oz) lean minced (ground) pork
75 g (2½ oz) fresh white breadcrumbs (not the dried variety)
2 teaspoons finely chopped fresh oregano (or 1 teaspoon dried)
1 onion, coarsely grated
1 garlic clove, finely grated
grated zest of 1 lemon
1 egg, beaten
1 teaspoon sea salt
2 tablespoons olive oil
plain (all-purpose) flour, for dusting
25 g (¾ oz) grated pecorino (or any other hard or semi-hard Italian cheese)
freshly ground black pepper

Roasted passata
500 ml (18 fl oz/2¼ cups) passata (sieved tomatoes)
1 teaspoon soft light brown sugar
2 garlic cloves, left whole but peeled
3 sprigs of thyme
1 onion, halved
30 g (1 oz) unsalted butter, roughly chopped

To make the meatballs, put the minced pork in a mixing bowl. Add the breadcrumbs, oregano, onion, garlic, lemon zest, egg, salt and a grind of black pepper. Mix together with your hands until combined. Fry a teaspoon of the mixture in a little oil, to check the seasoning and adjust accordingly.

Wet your hands (to stop the mixture from sticking) and shape it into 8 large meatballs, about 95 g (3 oz) each. Arrange the meatballs on a plate and chill for about 30 minutes so they firm up a little.

For the roasted passata, preheat a fan oven to 180°C (350°F/gas 6). Pour the passata into an ovenproof dish and stir in the sugar, peeled garlic cloves and thyme. Place the onion halves cut-side down in the sauce, then scatter the butter over the top. Season with salt and pepper and roast for 30 minutes, stirring halfway and scraping any nice jammy bits from around the edges back into the sauce.

Heat the oil in an ovenproof frying pan (skillet) over a medium-high heat. Dust the meatballs in a little flour then put them in the hot oil and fry for a couple of minutes on each side until golden (don't worry if they're not fully cooked at this stage as they're going back into the oven). If there's a lot of excess oil in the pan, spoon some out.

When the tomato sauce is ready, discard the onion and thyme and mash the garlic into the sauce using the back of a fork. Spoon or pour the sauce over the meatballs, then return to the oven for 10 minutes. Sprinkle over the cheese and bake for another 10 minutes until golden. Serve with chunks of bread and a green salad.

—

NOTES ON… ROASTED TOMATO SAUCE
The inspiration for my roasted passata comes from the Italian writer Marcella Hazan. I love the no-nonsense method of roasting tinned tomatoes or passata with aromatics to intensify the flavour. It's much easier than reducing the sauce on the hob when its lava-like simmer can make a mess. I usually make a huge batch and pop any leftover in the freezer, ready for meatballs, to spoon over pasta, or to poach eggs in.

Apparently, this fish stew was originally made by Italian immigrants who settled in San Francisco. After work, they would stop by the fishing boats on the wharf and collect any leftovers from the day's catch to cook up at home. In San Francisco you'll often find crab and scallops in the mix, but prawns, white fish and mussels are a more economical option. Along with fresh tomatoes, caramelised fennel and white wine they create a delicate and subtle fish stew. You can happily substitute dry vermouth for white wine, if you prefer. Serve this stew with few dollops of aioli or mayonnaise (page 183) and plenty of crusty bread to mop up the juices.

SERVES: 4
PREP: 15 mins
COOK: 40 mins

CIOPPINO
—

fisherman's stew

1 tablespoon olive oil
1 tablespoon unsalted butter
2 onions, diced
1 fennel bulb, diced (fronds reserved and core discarded)
2 garlic cloves, sliced
2 fresh bay leaves
½ teaspoon sweet smoked paprika, plus extra to serve
100 ml (3½ fl oz/scant ½ cup) white wine
250 g (9 oz) ripe tomatoes, roughly chopped
250 ml (8½ fl oz/1 cup) fresh fish stock
4 × 100 g (3½ oz) fresh hake fillets (or any other firm white fish)
8 raw tiger prawns (shrimp)
150 g (5 oz) mussels, cleaned and any open shells discarded
lemon juice, to taste (optional), plus wedges
handful of chopped flat-leaf parsley
sea salt and freshly ground black pepper

Heat the oil and butter in a large sauté pan or casserole dish (Dutch oven) over a medium-low heat, add the onions and fennel with a good pinch of salt and sweat for 5 minutes (don't season again until you've added the seafood as it may be salty in itself). Add the garlic and bay and sweat gently for another 15–20 minutes, stirring regularly, until everything is soft, translucent and turning golden.

Add the paprika and fry for 1 more minute, then add the wine and simmer for 2–4 minutes to bubble off the alcohol. Add the tomatoes, fry for another 2–3 minutes, then add the fish stock to the dish and bring to a gentle simmer. (You can set the dish aside at this stage, then reheat when you're ready to continue.)

Nestle the fish, prawns and mussels into the gently simmering sauce, grind over some black pepper and cover the pan with a lid (or use a sheet of kitchen foil topped with a large plate or chopping board). Uncover after 6 minutes and check everything is cooked through. If not, recover and check after another 2 minutes.

To serve, remove the lid and discard any unopened mussels. Check the seasoning: it may benefit from a little salt and a firm squeeze of lemon juice. Serve scattered with the parsley, the reserved chopped fennel fronds and some lemon wedges.

—

NOTES ON… SWEATING VEGETABLES
For this dish it really is worth taking your time over frying the onion, fennel and garlic. Frying gently over a low heat allows the vegetables to soften and turn translucent, before turning golden as their sugars caramelise. I tend to use a large frying pan (skillet) or sauté pan with a wide base and a tight-fitting lid, covering the pan with a lid at the beginning if they start to colour too quickly. If you don't have a lid, you can add a splash of water to the pan, which will help to soften the vegetables without colouring too quickly.

SERVES: 6
PREP: 25 mins
+ cooling
COOK: 30 mins

I love how in California you often see chicken liver pâté paired with preserved lemons (see picture on opposite page) rather than cornichon pickles, which is more common in Europe. I suppose the sharp, cleansing qualities of both have the same effect against the richness of the liver.

CHICKEN LIVER TOASTS

—

with fig and preserved lemon

400 g (14 oz) chicken livers
60 g (2 oz) unsalted butter
1 onion, finely chopped
75 g (2½ oz) figs (2 small or 1 large),
   finely chopped
1 heaped teaspoon thyme leaves
pinch of ground allspice
50 ml (2 fl oz/3 tablespoons)
   Manzanilla sherry
2 tablespoons water
3 tablespoons sour cream
1 teaspoon lemon juice
caster (superfine) sugar,
   to taste (optional)
sea salt and freshly ground
   black pepper

To serve
2 × ¼ pieces of preserved lemon
   (for homemade version see page 25)
6 slices of charred sourdough
   (for method see page 24)
½ teaspoon pink peppercorns,
   crushed
2 figs, quartered

Chicken livers can have quite a lot of gristle, so cut away and discard any stringy bits from the middle and chop into 3 cm (1¼ in) pieces. Pat dry with paper towels and season with salt and pepper.

Heat a large, heavy frying pan (skillet) over a medium-high heat. Add half the butter and, when foaming, carefully add the livers. Sear on one side for 2 minutes, then fry, stirring occasionally, for another 2 minutes: they should be golden on the outside and still a little pink in the middle. Lift out of the pan with tongs and set aside on a plate.

Return the pan to a medium heat (along with any remaining butter and bits of fried liver stuck to the pan). Add another 15 g (½ oz) of butter and the onion. Season with salt and fry for about 15 minutes, stirring occasionally, until golden and caramelised. Add the figs, thyme and allspice and sauté for 2 minutes. Return the chicken livers to the pan, pour in the sherry and cook for 2–3 minutes until reduced and everything is coated in a sticky sauce. Remove from the heat and set aside to cool for 15 minutes.

Tip everything into a small blender or food processor with the water, sour cream and remaining butter. Blitz until smooth. Check the seasoning. You can serve it immediately, but it definitely benefits from overnight chilling so the flavours have time to develop. Tip it into a bowl, (pass it through a sieve/fine mesh strainer if grainy) cover the surface of the pâté with cling film (plastic wrap) and chill.

When ready to serve, scoop out and discard the flesh from the two quarters of preserved lemon, then thinly slice the rind.

I like to serve some toasts already made up: spread with paté and scattered with preserved lemon rind (plus a few drops of the pickling liquid) and crushed pink peppercorns. I spoon the rest of the paté into a bowl, spreading it with the back of the spoon around the edges, and serve it alongside quartered figs, more preserved lemon, peppercorns and toast.

California Living + Eating

I've eaten mind-blowingly good pizza in California, just as good as any I've had in Italy. But I think the point of difference is the toppings. There's that charming Californian freedom that means you find all sorts of different adornments that you mightn't see on more traditional menus. This recipe is for pizzette, which are just smaller pizzas (I tend to serve one per person on a table filled with other salads). I don't have a pizza oven or any special equipment, so this recipe is totally achievable in any domestic kitchen. I encourage you to play with toppings, though for me some sliced fennel salami and a few slices of fried courgette are all I need. The only thing I would strongly advise is not to overload them; the lighter you go with the toppings, the better the pizzette tend to turn out.

MAKES: 6
PREP: 1 hr +
overnight proving
COOK: 40 mins

PIZZETTE

500 g (1 lb 2 oz) strong white
   bread flour, plus extra for dusting
¼ teaspoon (2 g) easy bake yeast
2 teaspoons fine sea salt
2 tablespoons extra virgin olive oil,
   plus extra for greasing
310 ml (11 fl oz/1⅓ cups)
   warm water

Raw tomato sauce
400 g (14 oz) fresh tomatoes,
   roughly chopped (or a 400 g/
   14 oz tin good-quality plum
   tomatoes)
1 garlic clove
1 tablespoon extra virgin olive oil
½ teaspoon sea salt

To top the pizzette
125 g (4 oz) ball mozzarella, drained
   and torn into about 18 small pieces
3–4 slices of finocchiona
   (fennel salami), cut into strips
   (optional)
1 yellow courgette (zucchini),
   sliced and fried in a little olive oil
   (optional)
handful of basil leaves
Parmesan, for grating
extra virgin olive oil, for drizzling
sea salt and freshly ground
   black pepper

To make the dough, place the flour, yeast and salt in a large mixing bowl and stir to combine (or use a stand mixer with a dough hook). Make a well in the middle and pour in the olive oil, then the warm water. Mix to make a ball of soft, pillowy dough, adding a little more water if it's too dry, or flour if it's too wet.

Place the dough on a lightly oiled surface and knead for about 10 minutes until smooth and elastic (or 5 minutes in a mixer). Place in a large, oiled resealable freezer bag and chill overnight for 12–24 hours.

When you're ready to make the pizzette take the chilled dough out of the refrigerator and allow it to warm up for an hour. Divide the dough into 6 equal pieces (about 140 g/5 oz each) and with lightly floured hands, roll each into a smooth ball. Place on a sheet of baking parchment, cover with a piece of oiled cling film (plastic wrap) and leave to prove at room temperature for 1 hour.

Now make the tomato sauce. Put the tomatoes, oil, garlic and salt in a small blender or food processor and blitz until smooth. If using fresh tomatoes, pour through a fine sieve (fine-mesh strainer), allowing the excess tomato water to drain off (save it to add to soups or salad dressings). Have all your topping ingredients ready to go.

Preheat the oven to maximum and place a flat baking sheet on the top shelf. Tear 6 pieces of baking parchment, each big enough to hold a 20 cm (8 in) pizza.

One at a time, take a ball of dough and stretch it over your knuckles to form a 20 cm (8 in) circle. Or stretch it a little over your knuckles, then lay it on the parchment and push it around the edges using your fingertips so you have a thin middle and a thicker edge at the crust. Spread each circle of dough with 1 tablespoon of tomato sauce and scatter with about 3 small pieces of mozzarella, plus any toppings of your choice. Scatter with a few basil leaves, grate over a little Parmesan , drizzle over some extra oil and sprinkle with black pepper. Lift up the parchment and carefully slide it on to the hot baking sheet. Bake for 6–8 minutes, starting to prepare the next pizzette as soon as it goes into the oven (unless you have enough space to cook two at a time).

CALIFORNIA PIZZA

The story of what has come to be known as 'California pizza' starts in the 1980s, just as California cuisine was starting to really define itself, with chef Ed LaDou. LaDou was working in a restaurant called Prego in the Bay Area of California where he had mastered the art of making Neapolitan pizza, turning out thin crusty bases from the restaurant's wood-burning ovens.

But, while LaDou followed traditional techniques with his crusts, his approach to the sauces and toppings was quite different. He looked at all the wonderful produce around him in the restaurant kitchen and questioned why they couldn't go on a pizza. And when he served up a pizza of red (bell) pepper, ricotta, mustard and pâté to a customer, it was quite a game-changer.

The customer turned out to be chef Wolfgang Puck, now widely regarded as a pioneer of the California food revolution. Austrian-born and French-trained, Puck moved to the States in his early 20s and opened Spago in 1982. The restaurant became a celebrity haunt and quickly made him a household name, and it remains open today, having reached legendary status in the Los Angeles restaurant scene.

After eating LaDou's ingenious pizza, Puck quickly brought him to LA to the kitchens of Spago. Today you can still eat the pizzas LaDou invented back in the 1980s – most famously the smoked salmon pizza with dill, crème fraîche and caviar (the base is warm, the topping is cold and there are no traditional cheese and tomato elements as such).

To me, this story encapsulates what I love so much about cooking in California: the freedom that chefs have to be daring and creative, and to play with traditional foods (though that's not to say, in my opinion, that some of the more international toppings went a touch too far). LaDou's legacy lives on. In the many places I have eaten great pizza in California – at Gjelina and Pizzeria Mozza in LA and at Delfina and Flour + Water in San Francisco to mention just a few – there's a breadth and panache that extends beyond more traditional toppings. And I admit to rather enjoying the likes of squash blossom, pickled padron peppers, caramelised fennel, grilled radicchio, braised short rib and lamb sausage adorning my pizza (though perhaps not all at once!).

In the States, sea bass is known by its Italian name, branzino, and although it is mainly a European fish you still see it a lot. I love sea bass. It's delicate, not too boney and it's very easy and quick to cook whole, either in the fan oven (20 minutes at 180°C/350°F/gas 6) or on the barbecue. This is great with Parmesan-crusted Cauliflower (page 180), though a green salad and some boiled new potatoes are just as good. The shallot vinaigrette goes perfectly with the white fish, though I would happily spoon it over tuna, salmon or chicken too.

SERVES: 2
PREP: 10 mins +
cooling time
COOK: 30 mins

BARBECUED SEA BASS

—

with shallot vinaigrette

2 whole sea bass (branzino),
   gutted, scaled and cleaned
   (you can also use sea bream
   or whole mackerel)
½ lemon, sliced
handful of thyme sprigs
sea salt

Shallot vinaigrette
90 ml (3 fl oz/generous ⅓ cup)
   extra virgin olive oil
1 banana shallot, thinly sliced
2 garlic cloves, halved
2 sprigs of thyme
1 tablespoon sherry vinegar
1 tomato, diced
1 tablespoon chopped chives
1 tablespoon chopped flat-leaf parsley

Start making the vinaigrette in advance. Put the oil, shallot, garlic and thyme in a small, cold saucepan with a good pinch of salt. Place over a low heat and allow all the ingredients to warm up gently. The aim is to poach the shallot in the oil over a very low heat for about 20 minutes, with just a few bubbles coming up now and then. The shallot and garlic should soften but take on no colour. After 20 minutes, take the pan off the heat, stir in the vinegar and leave to cool completely.

Heat a barbecue or a griddle pan over a medium heat. Cut 3 slits down each side of the fish, through the skin and flesh but not quite down to the bone, and stuff the cavities with the lemon and thyme. Cook on each side for 3–4 minutes, then check that the flesh is cooked – it should be opaque and come away from the bone. If you're unsure, you can always pop it into a 160°C (320°F/gas 4) fan oven for 5 minutes.

To finish the vinaigrette, discard the thyme and garlic and stir in the diced tomato and herbs. Spoon the vinaigrette over the cooked fish and serve.

California Living + Eating

SERVES: 4
PREP: 25 mins
COOK: 2 hrs

I first used coffee as a marinade for rib-eye steak a few years ago, and was pleasantly surprised at how its intensity and earthiness penetrated and flavoured the meat so well. It's just as good here, mellowed with maple syrup and soy sauce, and used as a braising liquor in which to cook the pork, which is then simmered down to a sticky glaze. I don't often eat pork belly as it's such a rich meat, but trimming off the top layer of skin and fat and serving a smaller portion with a heap of sharp pickled carrot and punchy sprouts gives balance. You can buy ready-trimmed slices or cut your own. I almost always make white basmati rice, whatever the dish, but choose whatever you prefer – brown, jasmine, long grain.

MAPLE, CHILLI + ESPRESSO PORK BELLY
—

with charred sprouts and pickled carrot

8 × 2–3 cm (¾–1¼ in) thick slices
   of trimmed pork belly (about 800 g/
   1 lb 12 oz)

Maple, chilli and espresso marinade
2 garlic cloves, crushed
200 ml (7 fl oz/scant 1 cup) espresso
   or strong coffee, cooled
2 tablespoons soy sauce
2 tablespoons sherry vinegar
4 tablespoons maple syrup
½ teaspoon chilli (hot pepper) flakes

Pickled carrot
5 medium carrots, shredded with
   a julienne peeler (about 300 g/
   10½ oz prepared weight)
3 tablespoons Japanese rice vinegar
2 teaspoons maple syrup
good pinch of sea salt

To serve
Charred Sprouts (page 181)
500 g (1lb 2 oz/2¾ cups) cooked rice
   (from about 185 g/6½ oz/1 cup)
   uncooked rice)
toasted sesame seeds (see method
   on page 25)

Mix all the marinade ingredients in a medium casserole dish (Dutch oven). Lower the prepared pork belly slices into the marinade, turning to coat if they're not fully submerged. Marinate for 1 hour at room temperature (if you have time, but don't worry if not).

Preheat a fan oven to 140°C (280°F/gas 3). Cover the casserole dish with a lid, place in the oven and cook for 1 hour 30 minutes.

Meanwhile, make the pickled carrot. Toss the shredded carrot in a bowl with the vinegar, maple syrup and salt. Chill until ready to serve, regularly tossing the carrot in the pickling mixture.

After 1 hour 30 minutes, remove the casserole dish from the oven and lift out the meat from the marinade; the slices should be soft and tender. Set the pork aside on a plate. Place the pan with the marinade on the hob and let it bubble over a medium-high heat until reduced to a loose glaze consistency; set aside.

Cook the rice and the sprouts. Finishing the pork will be the last thing you do before serving, so when you're ready (and the rice and sprouts are cooked), heat the grill (broiler) to high (240°C/460°F), or heat a griddle pan or barbecue over medium-high heat.

Brush the pork belly slices with some of the glaze and cook for about 3 minutes on one side, then brush them all over with more glaze and cook on the other side for another 3 minutes. Brush with a little more glaze so they're sticky and glossy all over.

Divide the warm rice between 4 bowls, top it with the drained pickled carrot, the sprouts and the sticky pork belly. Spoon over any remaining glaze, scatter with toasted sesame seeds and serve.

My sister Katja, who is a professional (and very talented) chef first made a version of this dish for me. It was delicate and fragrant, and quite different to what I expect from a plate of pasta. When she told me the ingredients included lemongrass and coriander I baulked a little, as I've always tried to be as classically Italian with my pasta sauces as possible. But actually it was an inspired combination and, exemplified the boldness of California cuisine. Plus, she used angel hair pasta (aka spaghettini) which I first remember eating with a simple tomato sauce in LA when I was about 9 years old.

SERVES: 2
PREP: 10 mins
COOK: 15 mins

ANGEL HAIR PASTA

—

with tiger prawns, lemongrass and coriander

2 lemongrass stalks, tender ends
   finely chopped (see below)
4 tablespoons olive oil
2 garlic cloves, thinly sliced
¼ teaspoon chilli (hot pepper) flakes
150 g (5 oz) raw, shelled tiger prawns
   (shrimp), roughly chopped (each
   into about 3 pieces)
juice of ½ lemon, plus extra wedges
   to serve
180 g (6 oz) angel hair pasta
   or spaghettini
handful of roughly chopped
   coriander (cilantro)
sea salt and freshly ground
   black pepper

Tip the chopped lemongrass into a cold medium sauté pan, add the oil, garlic and a good pinch of salt and set over a medium-low heat. As the oil warms up from cold, it will gently cook the garlic and lemongrass. Meanwhile, bring a separate saucepan of salted water to simmer ready to cook the pasta.

After about 5 minutes, or when the lemongrass and garlic fragrant and are just starting to turn golden, add the chilli flakes and chopped prawns. Add a pinch more salt and black pepper and continue cooking over a low heat for another 2–3 minutes until the prawns are cooked through. Add the lemon juice and take the pan off the heat.

Cook the spaghettini in the simmering water (check timings on the packet and cook for 1 minute less than suggested). Just before draining, reserve a cup of the cooking water.

Return the pan of prawns to the heat, toss in the pasta and a good splash of the reserved cooking water. Turn the strands of pasta gently with tongs until they are coated in a glossy sauce. Toss in the coriander and serve immediately, with extra lemon wedges.

—

NOTES ON… LEMONGRASS

Fragrant and citrussy, lemongrass is a tropical grass commonly used in Asian cooking. The stalks can be quite tough at the base, so I use only the more tender ends in pasta dishes such as this one, or in curry pastes and stir fries, chopping them as finely as possible. Keep the woodier stalks for infusing stocks, soups and stews, bashing them lightly to release their oils. Or slice them into thick chunks and brew in hot water for lemongrass tea, which is a refreshing and palate-cleansing way to end a meal.

California Living + Eating

CALIFORNIAN WINE

In much the same way that California's varied climate and diverse landscape are ideal for growing all sorts of fruit and vegetables, so too is its terroir ideal for grapes. Spanish missionaries planted the first vineyards in the 18th century solely for the purpose of making sacramental wine, but fast-forward 300 years and there are now near 3,500 wineries across the state, producing about 90 per cent of all US wine. California is also said to be the fourth biggest wine-growing region in the world, coming in behind France, Italian and Spain. And there was one seminal event that encouraged that to happen.

The Judgement of Paris was a blind wine tasting held in the French Capital in 1976, that pitched some of the finest whites from Burgundy and reds from Bordeaux against little-known Californian Chardonnays and Cabernet Sauvignons. None of the French judges believed the New World wines had a chance, but the results proved them wrong with many scoring the West Coast wines higher than those of their homeland. The story was picked up by *Time* magazine and California wine was proudly catapulted onto the international stage.

The wines that received the highest score at that Paris tasting – a 1973 Chardonnay from Chateau Montelena and a 1973 Cabernet Sauvignon from Stag's Leap Wine Cellar – both came from Napa. Which is perhaps unsurprising as Napa is the best-known of all of California's wine-growing regions, viewed internationally as a serious vinicultural playground. But nowadays there is far more to California wine than world-class cabernets and buttery chardonnays, and there are wine regions worth exploring throughout the state, running up and down the Pacific coast and throughout the central valley.

I've always had a huge soft spot for Sonoma, which lies to the west of Napa, just over some hills. It's bigger, more spread out and feels more laid back, where the wineries have bundles of character and are more far-reaching with their grape varieties. The food is outstanding too, and much of the recipe inspiration for this book was taken from fantastic meals eaten there. (I'll also never pass up a visit to Sonoma's Armstrong Redwoods State Natural Reserve to stand humbled amidst the awe-inspiring Redwood trees.)

Most recently, though, I spent time in the Central Coast wine region, which runs from south of San Francisco to north of Los Angeles. It immediately reminded me of that entrepreneurial energy that I love about California. 'There's a creative and collaborative spirit here,' master winemaker Damian Grindley of Brecon Estate explained to me. 'In a 20-mile radius we have so many different micro-climates, there's so much opportunity for the wine industry, there are over 300 varietals planted, we care about biodynamics and we've seen a lot of winemakers moving here from places like Napa to be a bit more experimental.' As he pours a beautifully light and crisp Albarino, a grape variety I've not seen grown in California before, his words ring true.

Although we tend to think of New York as the home of great Jewish food, I think the West Coast does delis pretty well too. I couldn't write a book without a recipe for Jewish chicken soup. It is, after all, the most nourishing, nurturing and comforting of foods. Plus, in essence, it is all about making a good stock, which I believe any good cook should make at least once it their lives. The stock recipe on page 24 is basically my mother's recipe for chicken soup, though she swears by adding parsley root. Sadly it is not always that easy to find, so a big handful of parsley leaves must suffice. I am rather pleased with my matzo balls here, too. After many attempts I think I have found a formula for light-and-fluffy-without-falling-apart balls.

**SERVES: 4
PREP: 10 mins +
30 mins chilling
COOK:
1 hr 25 mins**

JEWISH PENICILLIN

200 g (7 oz) medium matzo meal
¾ teaspoon sea salt
pinch of ground white pepper
heaped ½ teaspoon baking powder
2 eggs, separated
50 ml (2 fl oz/3 tablespoons) sunflower
    oil or schmaltz (chicken fat)
1.5 litres (50 fl oz/ 6¼ cups)
    homemade Chicken Stock, plus
    shredded leg meat (page 24)
handful of finely chopped
    flat-leaf parsley leaves
2 carrots, peeled and sliced into
    5 mm (¼ in) thick coins

Mix the matzo meal, salt, pepper and baking powder in a bowl.

Place the egg whites in a mixing bowl and use electric beaters to whisk until they form stiff peaks.

In a separate bowl, whisk the egg yolks and oil (or schmaltz) with a fork, then stir this into the matzo meal with 100 ml (3½ fl oz/scant ½ cup) of the chicken stock.

Fold in the egg whites until combined, then fold through the chopped parsley. Chill the mixture for 30 minutes.

Bring a large saucepan of water to the boil. Roll the matzo mixture into 8 balls, roughly 3–4 cm (1¼–1½ in) in diameter. Drop them into the boiling water, cover with a lid and simmer for 1 hour (you may need to top up with water towards the end of cooking), then remove with a slotted spoon.

Drain the water, rinse out the pan and add the stock. Bring to the boil, then simmer for 10 minutes. Add the carrot and simmer for another 10 minutes. Add the reserved chicken leg meat and the matzo balls and simmer for another 5 minutes. Ladle the soup, carrot and matzo balls into bowls and allow to cool a little before eating (I've burnt my tongue too many times, yet I never learn).

——

NOTES ON… SCHMALTZ
I have a thing for schmaltz (which is the just the Yiddish word for fat, but most commonly refers to chicken fat), so I always pour off any chicken fat that collects in the pan when I'm browning off chicken and chill it in a sealed jar. Then I use it for frying onions, or in the matzo ball recipe above instead of the oil.

SERVES: 2
PREP: 15 mins
COOK: 5 mins

This herb and pistachio pesto works really nicely with seared tuna steaks, but can also happily be spooned over roasted vegetables like broccoli and cauliflower. You can use any combination of soft herbs; I regularly mix it up and have yet to find a dud combination. Serve this with the Charred Cabbage with Chilli Lime Butter on page 171 or a simple green salad.

SEARED TUNA
—

with three-herb and pistachio pesto

California Living + Eating

Pesto
small handful of mint leaves
small handful of chives
large handful of coriander (cilantro),
   leaves and stalks
½ small garlic clove, finely grated
4 tablespoons extra virgin olive oil
20 g (¾ oz/2 tablespoons) toasted
   shelled pistachios (see method
   on page 25)
¼ piece of preserved lemon, rind
   thinly sliced (for homemade version
   see page 25)
2 tuna steaks (about 2 cm/¾ in thick)
1 tablespoon sunflower oil
sea salt

To make the pesto, put the herbs, garlic, olive oil and a pinch of salt in a small food processor and blitz until roughly chopped. Add the pistachios and preserved lemon rind and blitz again until the nuts are roughly chopped. Tip into a bowl and check the seasoning. Add a splash more oil or a little water to loosen the consistency. You can also add a little of the liquid from the jar of preserved lemons for sharpness.

Heat a large frying pan (skillet) over a high heat. Brush the tuna steaks with sunflower oil, season with salt and fry for 1–2 minutes on each side, depending on their thickness and how pink you want them in the middle. Remove from the pan and slice. Serve with the herbed pesto.

—

NOTES ON... GRATED GARLIC
When I read through all the recipes in this book before handing it into my publisher, I was shocked at how often I grate garlic into recipes. I am aware that raw garlic can make some people feel uneasy, but I use it as a seasoning, much like salt or lemon juice, to give depth and background flavour rather than letting anything taste overtly of raw garlic. I use a brilliant, fine Microplane grater that I've owned for years. It grates the garlic into a fine purée and allows me to grate in as little or as much I want. I often start with a little, building up more, to taste.

SERVES: 4
PREP: 15 mins
COOK: 50 mins

Orange chicken is often available at the hot deli counter at Erewhon, an organic foodstore in LA that I'm slightly besotted with. Their version is more like Chinese-style battered lemon chicken, and my version is a slightly more elegant take on it. This is a really undemanding dish that can be thrown together quickly for a weeknight supper and goes with pretty much anything: rice, mash and any veg. My sides of choice are the Cavolo Nero, Lemon and Fennel Salad (page 172) or the Broccoli, Bacon and Cranberry Slaw (page 163).

ORANGE CHICKEN

3 oranges, juice from 2 (about 150 ml/
   5 fl oz/scant ⅔ cup) and one sliced
1 tablespoon English mustard powder
2 tablespoons soy sauce
2 tablespoons soft light brown sugar
8 chicken thighs, skin-on
sea salt and freshly ground
   black pepper

To serve
cooked rice or mashed potato
   and greens

Preheat a fan oven to 180°C (350°F/gas 6).

Heat the orange juice in a small saucepan and bring to a simmer, then let it bubble until it has reduced by half.

Put the mustard powder in a bowl, then pour in the hot orange juice, stirring until the powder has dissolved. Add the soy sauce and sugar, mixing to combine.

Arrange the chicken skin-side up in a baking tray (pan). Pour the orange sauce over the chicken and baste the chicken a few times with the sauce. Season the chicken skin lightly with salt and pepper, then nestle the orange slices into the pan. Bake for 35 minutes, basting the chicken twice during cooking, until cooked through.

Serve the chicken with rice or mashed potato and plenty of greens.

In a land where fruit and vegetables are king, it's no surprise that the side orders are every bit as good as the main courses. These are bright and vivacious sides designed to furnish plates of simply grilled meat and fish, or to be served together as veggie sharing plates.

SIDES
+
SAUCES

California Living + Eating

SERVES: 4
PREP: 10 mins

It's hard to beat a really great tomato salad, and I think this is one. Tomatoes, soy sauce and nori are rich umami flavours and they truly complement each other, while the wasabi just adds a nice undercurrent of heat.

TOMATO, WASABI + NORI

500 g (1 lb 2 oz) tomatoes
(a mixture of colours and sizes)
1½ tablespoons sherry vinegar
1 tablespoon soy sauce
1 teaspoon groundnut (peanut) oil
1 teaspoon runny honey
1 teaspoon wasabi paste
½ sheet nori
handful of micro coriander (cilantro)
or chopped coriander leaves

Make sure your tomatoes are at room temperature (in general they should be stored at room temperature too, not in the refrigerator). Cut them into 1 cm (½ in) thick slices, cutting out any sections of thick core, and arrange over a serving plate. Whisk together the vinegar, soy, oil, honey and wasabi in a bowl. Taste and add more wasabi, if you like.

Spoon the dressing over the tomatoes. They can sit like this for a few minutes, but wait until you're ready to serve before sprinkling over the nori as it softens quickly. Cut the nori into 2 long strips about 2.5 cm (1 in) wide. Place the strips on top of each other and, using clean kitchen scissors, snip shards of nori over the tomatoes. Scatter over the coriander and serve immediately.

——

NOTES ON… MEASURING HONEY
This is a nifty trick I learned at culinary school: honey will stick to your measuring spoon, but if the spoon is coated with a little oil beforehand it will slide right off. So, if you're making a dressing which uses both ingredients, as above, then always measure out the oil first, following with the honey.

California Living + Eating

SERVES: 4
PREP: 15 mins +
30 mins draining

Grating beetroot (beet) can get a little messy, so wear gloves and an apron when making this. You can replace the same amount of beetroot with cucumber for a more traditional tzatziki.

BEETROOT TZATZIKI

California Living + Eating

200 g (7 oz) coarsely grated raw
    beetroot (beet) (from 3–4 medium
    raw, peeled beetroots)
1 teaspoon sea salt
150 g (5 oz) Greek yoghurt
½–1 small garlic clove, finely grated
squeeze of lemon juice
freshly ground black pepper
a few shredded mint leaves, to garnish

Put the grated beetroot in a bowl. Add the salt, mix it through and tip into a sieve (fine mesh strainer) then set over the bowl. Leave for at least 30 minutes for some of the excess liquid to drain off the beetroot.

In the sieve, press the grated beetroot with the back of a spoon to try to release more liquid, then tip into a large double layer of paper towel, wrap up and squeeze out over the sink trying to extract as much liquid as possible.

Tip into a clean mixing bowl with the yoghurt and garlic and mix together. You may want to add a little more yoghurt for a looser consistency. Season with a little lemon juice and a grinding of black pepper. Tip into a serving bowl and garnish with shredded mint leaves.

The globe artichoke seems to be the official vegetable symbol of California. They're very proud of their artichokes and Monterey (also famed for its aquarium, and being the location for Big Little Lies*) grows around 80 per cent of the artichokes that are eaten in the US. There's even an annual festival to celebrate them. Globe artichoke season runs from early to late summer. I think they make a wonderful light supper or a casual starter, and they really need little more than some lemon, butter and salt. When buying artichokes, look for pert green leaves that haven't browned at the edges.*

SERVES: 2
PREP: 5 mins
COOK: 35 mins

GLOBE ARTICHOKES

—

with lemon butter

California Living + Eating

2 globe artichokes
1 tablespoon lemon juice, plus an
    extra squeeze for the cooking water
75 g (2½ oz) unsalted butter
sea salt

Trim the artichoke stalks to just below the base and pull off the very tough leaves around the base. If the ends of the leaves are a little sharp and pointy, I like to trim the ends with a pair of scissors, too.

Bring a very large saucepan of water to the boil and add a good squeeze of lemon juice. Place the artichokes in the water, stem-side up. If they float up, keep them under the water with a heatproof plate topped with a heatproof weight.

Simmer for about 30 minutes (give large artichokes 35 minutes, and smaller ones 20–25 minutes). Drain and leave to cool, stem-side up, on a rack for 5 minutes.

For the sauce, you can simply melt the butter and stir in the lemon juice, with a pinch of salt. If you want to make an emulsified sauce, the put the lemon juice in a small pan over a low heat. Cut the chilled butter into cubes and whisk in a cube at a time, taking the pan off the heat if it gets too hot. Pour into a bowl, season with salt and pepper, and serve with the artichokes.

Pick off the leaves one by one, dipping the base of each leaf in the butter and scraping off the soft flesh at the base with your teeth. Once the leaves no longer yield any meat, pull them out until you reach the hairy choke. With a spoon, scoop out and discard the choke. Trim the base and any remaining tough leaves, and cut the choke into portions to dip in the sauce and eat.

SERVES: 2–3
PREP: 20 mins
COOK: 5 mins

I've spotted variations on this slaw in many places in California, but rarely seen anything like it in the UK. I like the idea of eating broccoli raw, it just needs to be broken down into tiny pieces to make it palatable. Then mixing it with bacon, cranberries and red onion makes it even more so.

BROCCOLI, BACON + CRANBERRY SLAW

3 slices smoked streaky bacon,
   cut into small 5mm (¼ in)
   thick strips
150 g (5 oz) broccoli florets
2 tablespoons dried cranberries
1 tablespoon finely diced red onion
2 tablespoons toasted sunflower seeds
   (see method on page 25)
2 tablespoons mayonnaise
   (for homemade version see
   page 183)
2 tablespoons Greek yoghurt
1 teaspoon lemon juice
½ teaspoon hot horseradish
sea salt and freshly ground
   black pepper

Put the bacon in a small frying pan (skillet) over a medium-low heat and fry for about 5 minutes until golden. Lift out with a slotted spoon and set aside to drain on paper towel.

You want really little pieces of broccoli for the slaw, about the size of the tip of your little finger. So, chop the broccoli into smallish florets, then break those into really small pieces with your hands; you'll end up not using a lot of the stem so keep this for juicing or a soup. Alternatively, pulse the broccoli in a food processor, until broken down into small pieces (you can leave the stem in if using a food processor).

Tip the broccoli into a large mixing bowl and add the cranberries, onion, bacon and sunflower seeds.

Mix the mayonnaise, yoghurt, lemon juice and horseradish in a bowl. Season with salt and pepper and stir half of this through the broccoli. You'll probably want to add a little more dressing, though it depends on how 'wet' you like your slaw.

California Living + Eating

SERVES: 4
PREP: 15 mins
COOK: 45 mins

This miso butter can be spooned over anything from grilled steak and roast chicken to green beans, but its saltiness has a real affinity with the candied orange flesh of sweet potato.

BAKED SWEET POTATOES

—

with miso butter and blistered peanuts

4 sweet potatoes
3 tablespoons (about 35 g/1¼ oz) unsalted peanuts
75 g (2½ oz) unsalted butter, softened
50 g (2 oz) white miso paste
juice of ½ lime
2 spring onions (scallions), thinly sliced
1 teaspoon toasted white sesame seeds (see method on page 25)

Preheat a fan oven to 180°C (350°F/gas 6).

Rinse the potatoes if they need it, then pierce them all over with a fork and place in a baking tray (pan) or large ovenproof dish. Bake for 45–55 minutes or until soft to the touch.

Toast the peanuts in a dry frying pan (skillet) for 5–6 minutes, tossing them regularly until blistered in places. Tip onto a chopping board to cool, then roughly chop.

Meanwhile, lightly beat the butter in a bowl with a spatula. You want it to be just light and fluffy. Beat the miso into the butter and set aside.

Once the potatoes are ready, remove them from the oven and split them in half. Fluff the middles with a fork and divide most of the miso butter between them, serving any extra on the side. Squeeze over the lime juice and scatter with the sliced spring onion, chopped peanuts and sesame seeds.

I've watched a huge number of diet fads come and go over the years, but the recent trend for a plant-based diet has more staying power. The idea that what we eat should predominantly come from a wide range of unprocessed and unrefined plant-based sources – fruit, veg, nuts, seeds, legumes and grains – is to my mind a good one. I also think there's room for meat, fish and dairy, as long as it comes from high-quality and high-welfare sources.

My time studying at Matthew Kenney Culinary school (which later became known as PlantLab) in Los Angeles in 2017 hugely influenced my approach to plant-based eating. Firstly, the school was situated on Abbot Kinney, a pretty parade of shops and restaurants just a few blocks back from Venice beach on the west side of the city. Here it is mind-blowingly easy to eat a plant-based diet and to eat it well. (Though in fairness this is true of other parts of LA, plus all the food on Abbot Kinney, plant-based or not, is good.)

The most valuable thing I learned was different ways of preparing produce. I made my first jar of kimchi at the school, which opened up the world fermentation to me and led to me developing a passion for water kefir (page 66). I blended cashews into wonderfully creamy sauces that anyone would think contained dairy; I pickled thinly sliced ginger with a dash of beetroot (beet) juice so it was fiery and pink; I made raw, vegan Caesar salad dressing out of blended sunflower seeds; and candied pumpkin seeds with maple syrup and tamari to scatter over salads. There were sushi rolls wrapped in sheets of daikon, flatbreads made purely of dehydrated vegetables and seeds, refined sugar-free granolas bolstered with sprouted buckwheat, and delicious chocolate ice cream made of little more than blended fresh coconut, cacao and maple syrup.

You won't find these exact recipes in this book (seek them out in Matthew Kenney's books) but you will find a handful of dishes that are directly inspired by my time there. The techniques, clever processes and the attention to detail I learned at his school influenced my cooking greatly. We don't all have the time or means to study this kind of cuisine, but there is a lot of information out there now about plant-based eating. Cooking for yourself regularly and taking the time to be creative and try something new is a good starting point.

PLANT-BASED EATING

SERVES: 2
PREP: 20 mins
COOK: 5 mins

This is a firecracker of a salad with tons of fresh herbs and flecks of hot chilli, though the lime and fresh coconut keep everything cool. You can buy fresh, shelled coconut quite easily nowadays, or have a go at cracking your own. I think this is best served with a piece of fish fresh off the barbecue.

FRESH COCONUT SALAD

—

with green beans

150 g (5 oz) green beans, trimmed
    and cut into 2 cm (¾ in) lengths
75 g (2½ oz) grated coconut (ideally
    on a medium-coarse grater, or a box
    grater will do)
150 g (5 oz) cherry tomatoes, halved
1 red birds eye chilli, very finely
    chopped (seeded if liked)
juice of 1 lime
1 teaspoon sunflower oil
Small handful chives, finely chopped
Small handful mint leaves,
    finely chopped
Small handful coriander (cilantro),
    finely chopped

Blanch the beans in a saucepan of boiling salted water for 2 minutes, then drain and rinse under the cold tap to cool. Add to the bowl with the coconut, tomatoes, chilli, lime juice and oil. Season with a pinch of salt and toss everything together. Stir through the herbs and serve immediately.

SERVES: 4
PREP: 25 mins
COOK: 5 mins

It saddens me that the cabbage I grew up eating was usually boiled. There are so many ways to prepare a cabbage to make it taste amazing and this is certainly one: charred in a pan and doused in chilli-lime butter.

CHARRED CABBAGE

—

with chilli-lime butter

1 hispi or pointed spring cabbage
50 g (2 oz) unsalted butter
1 small red chilli, thinly sliced
  (seeded if liked)
juice of ½ lime
sea salt

Trim the base of the cabbage, then cut the cabbage into thick wedges. Sprinkle with a little water, so it gets inside the leaves. This just helps it to steam a little on the inside when it's cooking. Heat a large frying pan (skillet) over a medium-high heat until it's nice and hot.

Heat the butter in a small saucepan. Brush a little butter over the cut sides of the cabbage, season with some salt and place cut side down in the hot frying pan. Cook for 3–4 minutes until golden in places, then turn each wedge onto the other cut-side and cook for another 3–4 minutes. Turn onto the rounded side and cook for a minute or so, until the wedges are nicely charred on all sides. Lift out of the pan and set aside on a platter.

Continue to heat the small pan of butter over a medium heat until bubbling and the milk solids start to turn golden and smell nutty. Take the pan off the heat, and add the chilli and lime juice. Spoon over the cabbage and serve immediately.

California Living + Eating

**SERVES: 2–3
PREP: 15 mins**

This is a really fresh and quite vegetal salad that provides a nice foil to richer meat dishes or oily fish. You can use any dried fruit instead of raisins or some orange segments can be tumbled in just before serving, too.

CAVOLO NERO, LEMON + FENNEL SALAD

10 g (⅓ oz) raisins
100 g (3½ oz) cavolo nero
1 small fennel bulb
1 tablespoon extra-virgin olive oil
juice of ½ small lemon
sea salt and freshly ground
   black pepper

Soak the raisins in a heatproof bowl of just-boiled water while you prepare the rest of the salad, so they soften and plump up a little.

Strip the leaves from the stalks of the cavolo nero (save the stalks to add to soups or smoothies). Finely shred the leaves and tip them into a bowl.

Cut any fronds from the fennel and set aside. Trim off any discoloured ends or tough outer layers, then finely shred the fennel, discarding the tough core (slice it on a mandoline if you have one). Tip into the bowl with the cavolo nero. Drain the raisins, roughly chop them, and add to the bowl.

When ready to serve, whisk together the oil and lemon juice, season with salt and pepper and toss with the salad and the reserved fennel fronds.

SERVES: 4
PREP: 15 mins
COOK: 10 mins

Using different colour courgettes (zucchinis) and preparing them two different ways makes for a bright and texturally interesting side dish, though if you can only find green courgette it will taste just as good.

COURGETTE, LEMON + PARMESAN SALAD

California Living + Eating

1 green courgette (zucchini),
   ends trimmed
1 yellow courgette (zucchini),
   ends trimmed
1 tablespoon olive oil
2 teaspoons toasted sunflower seeds
   (see method on page 25)
sea salt and freshly ground
   black pepper

Parmesan and lemon dressing
2 tablespoons extra virgin olive oil
2 tablespoons lemon juice
2 tablespoons finely grated Parmesan,
   plus a few extra shavings to garnish

Use a vegetable peeler to pare long strips of the green courgette (save the core and add it to soups or smoothies). Place in a large bowl of iced water (see Note on page 87, this helps the ribbons crisp up and stay firm once dressed, rather than wilt in the oil).

Slice the yellow courgette into coins just under 1 cm (½ in) thick. Toss in a bowl with the olive oil and season with salt and pepper. Heat a barbecue or griddle pan over a medium-high heat and cook the yellow courgette for 2–3 minutes on each side, until nicely charred and tender. Remove from the pan and allow to cool slightly.

Mix all the dressing ingredients together and season with a little salt and pepper. Don't worry if the Parmesan clumps a little in places.

Lift the green courgette ribbons from the water and drain them well on paper towel. Arrange on a serving plate with the grilled yellow courgette. Spoon over the dressing and scatter with the sunflower seeds and extra Parmesan shavings.

California Living + Eating

Pictured: Courgette, Lemon and Parmesan Salad (recipe opposite); Roasted Broccoli (page 178)

SERVES: 4
PREP: 15 mins
COOK: 15 mins

We all know just how good roasted cauliflower is, so give broccoli a chance too. It roasts up really nicely and is flexible enough to have all manner of sauces spooned over it. I sometimes serve it with yoghurt and chimmichurri, or a Caesar dressing, though a quick tahini and parsley sauce is the easiest to throw together at the last minute. (See photograph on page 177.)

ROASTED BROCCOLI

—

with green tahini

2 small broccoli heads
1–2 tablespoons olive oil
1 tablespoon tahini
2 tablespoons water
1 tablespoon lemon juice
½ teaspoon toasted sesame oil
¼ teaspoon maple syrup
½ garlic clove, finely grated
handful of chopped flat-leaf parsley
sea salt and freshly ground
    black pepper

Preheat a fan oven to 200°C (400°F/gas 7) and line a large baking tray (pan) with baking parchment.

Ideally you want to cut cross-sections of the broccoli, about 1–1.5 cm (½ in–⅔ in) thick, so try to do this by slicing through the head with a large knife. Don't worry about any of the florets that fall off, they'll all end up being roasted together.

Arrange all the broccoli over the lined baking tray and sprinkle with the oil, gently turning so it's coated all over. Season with salt and pepper and roast for 15 minutes, turning halfway.

Meanwhile, mix the tahini with the water, lemon juice, sesame oil and maple syrup in a bowl until smooth. Stir through the garlic and parsley and season with salt and pepper. Arrange the broccoli on a plate and spoon over the dressing.

SERVES: 4
PREP: 15 mins
COOK: 40 mins

I often serve these delicious nuggets of cauliflower on top of a Caesar salad instead of grilled chicken or prawns; the garlic and Parmesan in the breadcrumbs complement the dressing nicely. Alternatively, just eat them as a snack straight from the baking tray!

PARMESAN-CRUSTED CAULIFLOWER

1 cauliflower
3 tablespoons olive oil
5 tablespoons fresh white
   breadcrumbs
5 tablespoons grated Parmesan
1 garlic clove, crushed
grated zest of ½ lemon
1 tablespoon finely chopped
   flat-leaf parsley
sea salt and freshly ground
   black pepper

Preheat a fan oven to 180°C (350°F/gas 6) and line a baking tray (pan) with baking parchment.

Remove the outer leaves from the cauliflower and discard any thick, tough or discoloured leaves, but reserve any nice tender ones.

Cut out the tough core from the middle of the cauliflower, then cut or break the cauliflower into medium-sized florets. Toss them in a bowl with 2 tablespoons of the oil, arrange in the lined baking tray, season with salt and pepper and roast for 20 minutes, turning them halfway.

In a bowl, toss together the breadcrumbs, Parmesan, garlic, lemon zest and parsley. Season with salt and pepper and drizzle with the remaining tablespoon of oil, tossing to combine. Sprinkle the breadcrumbs over the cauliflower and roast for a final 10 minutes until golden.

SERVES: 4
PREP: 5 mins
COOK: 15 mins

It's worth taking time to pre-cook the sprouts before finishing them in the frying pan; it ensures they're tender in the middle. These are great with the Maple, Chilli and Espresso Pork Belly on page 142, but also make a punchy side for any grilled chicken and fish.

CHARRED SPROUTS
—

with fish sauce and sesame seeds

300 g (10½ oz) small Brussels
  sprouts, trimmed
1 tablespoon sunflower oil
1 tablespoon fish sauce
1 teaspoon maple syrup
juice of ½ lime
½ teaspoon toasted white sesame
  seeds (see method on page 25)

Pre-cook the sprouts before frying them. Either steam them for 3–4 minutes (this is the ideal method, as it avoids them getting too waterlogged), or plunge them into a saucepan of boiling water and simmer for 2–3 minutes before draining. After steaming or boiling the sprouts, refresh them immediately under the cold tap to retain their colour, then halve them and set aside to drain on paper towel.

To finish the sprouts, heat the oil in a large frying pan (skillet) until hot. Add the halved sprouts and fry for 2–3 minutes over a high heat until charred in places. Tip in the fish sauce and maple syrup and fry for another couple of minutes. Just before serving, squeeze over the lime juice and scatter over the sesame seeds.

California Living + Eating

**MAKES: 200 ml
(7 fl oz/scant 1 cup)
PREP: 5 mins**

MAYONNAISE

Homemade mayonnaise is far superior to any mayonnaise you can buy, even though there are some good options out there nowadays. I was taught the old-school way, using the prongs of a fork to add one drop of oil at a time to the yolks and whisking by hand. It's a good lesson in understanding how important it is to emulsify the two fats slowly, and is also relevant if you make it in a small food processor (adding the oil very slowly to start). Then I discovered a brilliant all-in-one method using an upright hand-held stick blender and a tall cup (which they usually come with when you buy them), meaning it's emulsified in literally seconds. As mayonnaise contains raw eggs, always use the freshest eggs you can find (I also use organic), and store leftovers in a sealed container in the refrigerator for no more than a few days.

1 egg yolk
pinch of cayenne pepper (optional)
pinch of English mustard powder
  (optional)
2 teaspoons lemon juice, plus more
  to taste
¼ teaspoon sea salt
pinch of ground white or black pepper
75 ml (2½ fl oz/5 tablespoons)
  light olive oil
100 ml (3½ fl oz/scant ½ cup)
  sunflower oil
2 tablespoons warm water

Put all the ingredients in the base of a tall cup. Use an upright hand-held stick blender to blitz everything until combined. Check the seasoning, adding more salt and lemon juice to taste.

This is a base mayonnaise recipe and the flavour can be adjusted in many ways to suit different dishes. For example, add the following ingredients before blitzing:

– *lemon mayo*: add more lemon juice and a little grated zest
– *aioli*: add half a crushed garlic clove
– *green chilli aioli*: add a chopped green chilli and half a crushed garlic clove
– *basil mayo*: add a handful of basil leaves
– *tomato mayo*: add 1–2 teaspoons tomato purée (paste)
– *mustard mayo*: add 1 tablespoon Dijon, wholegrain or English mustard

California Living + Eating

MAKES:
about 300 ml
(10 fl oz/1¼ cups)
PREP: 5 mins
COOK: 20 mins

I have seen more complex recipes for hot sauce, that include the likes of onions, red peppers and fish sauce, but this is a very simple and very delicious version. Of course, its heat will depend on your chillies. I don't mind if it turns out blow-the-roof hot; I just mix it with yoghurt or mayonnaise before eating to temper the heat. I have made this using other vinegars, but rice vinegar's lower acidity gives a finish that is less harsh and more rounded.

HOT SAUCE

10 red chillies
200 g (7 oz) tomatoes,
  roughly chopped
2 garlic cloves, roughly chopped
250 ml (8½ fl oz/1 cup)
  Japanese rice vinegar
2 teaspoons soft dark brown sugar
½ teaspoon sea salt

Trim the stalks off the chillies, then roughly chop them. I leave the seeds in but if you want a milder sauce I would suggest removing them (or remove them from half the chillies to retain some heat). Tip the chillies into a saucepan with the rest of the ingredients. Bring to the boil, then lower the heat and simmer for 15 minutes.

Allow to cool completely, then blitz in a high-speed blender (see page 23) until smooth. You may want to add a splash of water to give it a looser consistency – I usually add between 1–2 tablespoons. Tip into sterilised jars (see Preserved Lemons on page 25) and store in the refrigerator for up to a month

I do a lot of quick pickling – leaving vegetables to soak briefly in vinegar, salt and sugar – in this book. But I also think every refrigerator should have a big jar of proper pickles at the ready. This is a very basic pickle and you can vary the spices and veggies. I love pickled radish, though it does have a tendency to turn the whole jar 50 shades of pink. I once found white radishes which worked very well. I also use a small amount of sugar, as I like my pickles quite sharp. Increase it to 75 g (2½ oz/⅓ cup) if you prefer a little more sweetness.

MAKES: enough to fill a 1 litre (34 fl oz/4 cup) jar
PREP: 20 mins

HOUSE PICKLES

300 ml (10 fl oz/1¼ cups) cider vinegar
150 ml (5 fl oz/scant ⅔ cup) water
50 g (2 oz/¼ cup) golden caster (superfine) sugar
200 g (7 oz) cucumber, cut into spears
1 teaspoon sea salt
200 g (7 oz) carrots, cut into spears
150 g (5 oz) radishes, halved
2–3 sprigs of dill
2 fresh bay leaves
1 teaspoon fennel seeds
1 teaspoon coriander seeds

Sterilise your jar (see Preserved Lemons on page 25). Put the vinegar, water and sugar in a saucepan and heat until the sugar has dissolved, then set aside to cool completely.

Meanwhile, place the cucumber spears in a colander and toss with the salt. Set over a bowl and leave for 30 minutes so that any excess water can drain out (this helps to crisp up the cucumber, but is not necessary for the carrot).

Tip the cucumber, carrots and radishes into a sterilised jar, with the herbs and spices, and pour over the cooled pickling liquor. Seal and chill for 24 hours, then you can start eating them! They will keep for up to 1 month once opened.

The heady waft of freshly
baked cakes, cookies and tarts
emerging from the oven
is one that is hard to beat.

FULLY BAKED

I remember the first time I walked into Chez Panisse early one summer and immediately spotted a beautiful apricot galette sitting up on the counter. There was an effortless beauty about the way it looked, which I think is the essence of this recipe – a rudimentary combination of pastry and fruit. Sadly there are only a couple of weeks a year that you find good apricots in the UK, but I have made this recipe using them when they are available. It's actually adjustable to any fruit, though stone fruits have a particular affinity with the almondy pastry.

**SERVES: 8
PREP: 30 mins +
30 mins chilling
COOK: 30 mins**

CHERRY + ALMOND GALETTE

300 g (10½ oz) cherries, halved
  and stoned
1 teaspoon cornflour (cornstarch)
2 tablespoons caster (superfine) sugar
small squeeze of lemon juice
pinch of sea salt

Pastry
75 g (2½ oz) ground almonds
150 g (5 oz/1¼ cups) plain
  (all-purpose) flour, plus extra
  for dusting
2 tablespoons caster (superfine)
  sugar, plus an extra ½ tablespoon
  for scattering
pinch of fine sea salt
100 g (3½ oz) unsalted butter,
  cubed and chilled
a few drops of almond
  essence (optional)
2 tablespoons iced water
a little beaten egg, for glazing

To serve
single (light) cream, crème fraîche
  or vanilla ice cream

To make the pastry, pulse the almonds, flour, sugar and salt in a food processor to combine. Pulse in the butter until the mixture resembles breadcrumbs. Blitz in a few drops of almond essence (if using) and the iced water until it forms a ball. Turn the dough out onto the work surface and gently bring it together with your hands. Place on a large sheet of baking parchment and cover with another large sheet of parchment. Press out the dough with your hands to a circle roughly 20 cm (8 in) in diameter. Chill for 30 minutes (or longer on a hot day).

Preheat a fan oven to 160°C (320°F/gas 4) and put a large baking sheet in the oven to heat up.

Toss the cherries with the cornflour (to thicken up any excess juices and preventing the base of the pastry from becoming too wet), sugar, lemon juice and salt. (You may want to add more or less sugar depending on the sweetness of your fruit.)

Roll out the pastry between the parchment to make a circle about 30 cm (12 in) in diameter (roughly 3 mm (⅛ in) thick). Lift off the top layer of parchment.

Pile up the fruit in the middle of the pastry, aiming to leave a 5 cm (2 in) border. Bring the pastry edges up and around the fruit, leaving a gap in the middle so you can see the fruit. Brush the exposed pastry with a little beaten egg and sprinkle over the extra sugar.

Carefully slide the galette, still on the parchment, onto the hot baking sheet. Bake for about 30 minutes until the pastry is golden. Remove from the oven and cool for 10 minutes. Serve it warm or at room temperature with single cream, crème fraîche or vanilla ice cream.

NOTES ON… PASTRY
This pastry is easily made in a food processor. You can also make it by hand, by rubbing the butter into the flour and almonds, using your fingertips. Pastry likes a cool environment. If your kitchen is hot, the butter in the pastry will melt and it'll be hard to handle. Pop it in the refrigerator for 10 minutes to cool down.

SERVES: 4
PREP: 10 mins
COOK: 25 mins

Gjelina in Venice, Los Angeles is often hailed as being one of the great restaurants in which to eat true California cooking. Chef Travis Lett is a master of creating effortlessly elegant dishes, and this simple dessert is based on his strawberry-rhubarb polenta crisp. It is a glorious celebration of summer fruit, though you can adjust to whatever is seasonal – apple, pear and blackberry is a fine autumnal choice. You can add a little polenta (about 50 g/2 oz) into the crumble topping for added texture, too, just as they do at Gjelina.

RHUBARB, STRAWBERRY + OAT CRUMBLE

250 g (9 oz) rhubarb,
    cut into 1 cm (½ in) pieces
2 tablespoons water
1 tablespoon golden caster
    (superfine) sugar
200 g (7 oz) strawberries, sliced
50 g (2 oz/generous ¼ cup)
    soft light brown sugar
50 g (2 oz/scant ½ cup)
    plain (all-purpose) flour
50 g (2 oz) jumbo oats
pinch of fine sea salt
50 g (2 oz) unsalted butter,
    cubed and chilled

To serve
single (light) cream, crème fraîche
    or vanilla ice cream

Place the rhubarb, water and caster sugar in a small saucepan, place over a medium heat and simmer for 2 minutes. Tip into the base of a small-medium baking dish (about 1 litre/34 fl oz/4 cups in volume), or into smaller, individual ovenproof dishes, allow to cool, then stir in the strawberries.

Preheat a fan oven to 180°C (350°F/gas 6). Put the brown sugar, flour and oats in a mixing bowl with the salt. Add the butter and rub together with your fingertips to make a wet, clumpy crumble, then sprinkle over the fruit, piling it slightly higher in the middle. Bake for 20 minutes. Serve with single cream, crème fraîche or vanilla ice cream.

———

NOTES ON... UNSALTED BUTTER
I use unsalted butter in all my cooking because it means I can control how much salt goes into my food (different salted butters will have different salt contents). I do, however, always add salt to my sweet dishes as it's essential to help bring out the flavours. Likewise, a little sweetness is often beneficial in savoury dishes.

California Living + Eating

**MAKES: 12
PREP: 15 mins +
30 mins chilling
COOK: 15 mins**

Tahini (sesame paste) elevates these beyond the average cookie. I don't think it's necessary to use an expensive chocolate with a high percentage of cocoa in cookies. A slightly sweeter plain chocolate is fine and I like to leave the chunks quite large. I also use strong white bread flour in my cookies as it has a higher gluten content and gives a slightly chewier finish, but if you only have plain (all-purpose) flour they'll work just fine, too.

SESAME CHOCOLATE CHUNK COOKIES

100 g (3½ oz) unsalted butter
75 g (2½ oz) tahini
100 g (3½ oz/generous ½ cup)
  soft light brown sugar
75 g (2½ oz/scant ⅓ cup) golden
  caster (superfine) sugar
1 egg
170 g (6 oz/1⅓ cups) strong
  white bread flour
½ teaspoon fine sea salt
½ teaspoon bicarbonate of soda
  (baking soda)
100 g (3½ oz) plain chocolate,
  cut into chunks
1 tablespoon toasted white
  sesame seeds (see method
  on page 25)

Heat the butter and tahini in a saucepan until melted, stirring to combine, then set aside to cool slightly.

Beat in both the sugars using a wooden spoon, then beat in the egg. Combine the flour, salt and bicarbonate of soda and beat into the wet ingredients until combined. Finally, fold in the chocolate chunks. Chill the mixture for 30 minutes.

Preheat a fan oven to 160°C (320°F/gas 4) and line a large baking sheet with baking parchment.

Scoop heaped spoonfuls of the mixture and roll them lightly in your hands (you should get 12 heaped spoonfuls in total). Place the sesame seeds in a bowl and one at a time, dip each cookie dough ball into the seeds. Arrange them on the parchment, well spaced apart (you may need to bake them in batches) and press down lightly to flatten.

Bake for 10–12 minutes until spread and golden. Remove from the oven and leave to cool on the baking sheet for 5 minutes, then use a spatula to transfer them to a wire rack to cool completely.

SERVES: 8–10
PREP: 20 mins +
cooling
COOK: 55 mins

This is a very simple dairy-free carrot cake with the addition of coconut (desiccated inside, flakes on top). You can find really good dairy-free coconut milk yoghurts in many supermarkets now and they make an easy alternative to traditional cream cheese frosting, plus they aren't nearly as sweet.

CARROT + COCONUT CAKE

California Living + Eating

120 ml (4 fl oz/½ cup) sunflower oil, plus extra for greasing
3 eggs, separated
150 g (5 oz/generous ¾ cup) soft light brown sugar
100 g (3½ oz/generous ¾ cup) plain (all-purpose) flour
1½ teaspoons ground cinnamon
½ teaspoon ground ginger
1 teaspoon baking powder
1 teaspoon bicarbonate of soda (baking soda)
½ teaspoon fine sea salt
200 g (7 oz) coarsely grated carrot (about 3 large carrots)
100 g (3½ oz/generous cup) desiccated (dried shredded) coconut
grated zest of ½ orange

Topping
15 g (½ oz) coconut flakes
250 g (9 oz) non-dairy coconut milk yoghurt
2 tablespoons icing (confectioners') sugar
½ teaspoon vanilla bean paste

Preheat a fan oven to 160°C (320°F/gas 4). Grease a 900 g (2 lb) loaf tin (pan) and line it with baking parchment.

Place the egg whites in one mixing bowl and the yolks in another. Using electric beaters, whisk the egg whites until they form stiff peaks, then set aside.

Add the sugar to the mixing bowl with the egg yolks and whisk together with the beaters (there's no need to clean them after the whisking the egg whites). Slowly whisk in the oil, then the flour, spices, raising agents and salt.

Use a spatula or large spoon to fold in the grated carrot, coconut and orange zest, then fold through the egg whites until everything is combined. Tip into the loaf tin, then bake for 50–55 minutes or until a skewer inserted into the middle of the cake comes out clean. Remove from the oven and leave to cool completely in the pan on a wire rack.

Place the coconut flakes for the topping on a small roasting tray and bake for 2–3 minutes (watch them like a hawk as they can burn very quickly) until lightly golden, then set aside.

Just before serving, use a balloon whisk to whisk together the yoghurt, icing sugar and vanilla bean paste. Spread over the top of the cooled cake and sprinkle with the toasted coconut flakes.

——

NOTES ON… LINING A LOAF TIN (PAN)
You can buy very good loaf tin liners nowadays that slot straight into the tins. If you don't have these, however, grease the sides and base of the tin lightly with softened butter or oil, then cut a long strip of baking parchment the width of the tin and nestle it into the base and up the ends, leaving some overhang. The overhanging parchment helps you to lift out the cake when it's done, though do run a knife along the sides beforehand to make sure it hasn't stuck.

After baking many many batches, I finally achieved the right texture with these cookies, a nice crunch at the edges but chewy and sticky within. It's the amount of sugar that helps to create this texture. You can reduce it slightly, but the result is a bit more cakey (though the flavour just as good). I suppose these are a take on oatmeal raisin cookies, though the dates work really nicely. And they grow on glorious palm trees all over Palm Desert in southern California, as pictured opposite.

**MAKES: about 9 large cookies
PREP: 15 mins +
30 mins chilling
COOK: 15 mins**

MEDJOOL DATE + JUMBO OAT COOKIES
—

with flaky sea salt

100 g (3½ oz) unsalted butter
75 g (2½ oz/generous ⅓ cup)
   soft dark brown sugar
60 g (2 oz/¼ cup) golden caster
   (superfine) sugar
100 g (3½ oz) pitted medjool dates,
   roughly chopped
75 g (2½ oz/generous ½ cup)
   strong white bread flour,
   plus extra for dusting
125 g (4 oz) jumbo oats
½ teaspoon bicarbonate of soda
   (baking soda)
½ teaspoon flaky sea salt, plus extra
   for sprinkling on top
½ teaspoon ground cinnamon
1 egg
½ teaspoon vanilla extract

In a medium saucepan, warm the butter and sugars until the butter has melted, stirring to combine, then remove from the heat and leave to cool for 5 minutes.

Toss the dates in the flour with your fingers – this helps to stop them sticking together and allows you to break up any larger chunks. Stir in the oats, bicarbonate of soda, salt and cinnamon.

Using a wooden spoon, beat the egg and vanilla into the butter and sugar (you can do this in the saucepan), then stir the mixture into the dry ingredients until combined. Chill for 30 minutes.

Preheat a fan oven to 150°C (300°F/gas 3) and line a large baking sheet with baking parchment.

Dust your hands with a little flour. Take large spoonfuls of the mixture and roll them quickly in your hands (you should get 9 large spoonfuls in total). Arrange them on the parchment-lined sheet (you may need to cook them in 2 batches), well spaced apart. Sprinkle with a tiny bit more salt (or leave it off if you don't want them too salty).

Bake for 13–15 minutes, turning the baking sheet halfway if they are browning more on one side than the other, until spread and golden. Remove from the oven and leave to cool on the baking sheet for 5 minutes, then use a spatula to transfer them to a wire rack to cool completely.

California Living + Eating

These are unashamedly sweet and sticky, and by far the most indulgent recipe in this entire book. The dough is not disimilar to the breakfast buns on page 42 (where I give instructions for kneading by hand), but use plain (all-purpose) flour rather than strong white flour for a softer, more cake-like crumb.

MAKES: 9
PREP: 30 mins +
up to 3 hrs proving
COOK: 35 mins

STICKY PECAN BUNS

—

with maple caramel sauce

175 ml (6 fl oz/¾ cup) whole
   (full-fat) milk
100 g (3½ oz) unsalted butter
500 g (1 lb 2 oz/4 cups) plain
   (all-purpose) flour, plus extra
50 g (2 oz/generous ¼ cup)
   soft dark brown sugar
2 teaspoons (7 g/¼ oz) easy
   bake yeast
1 teaspoon ground cinnamon
1 teaspoon fine sea salt
2 eggs, lightly beaten
1 teaspoon vanilla bean paste
   or extract

Mapel caramel sauce
100 g (3½ oz) unsalted butter
100 g (3½ oz/generous ½ cup)
   soft dark brown sugar
200 ml (7 fl oz/scant 1 cup)
   double (heavy) cream
100 ml (3½ fl oz/scant ½ cup)
   maple syrup
1 teaspoon fine sea salt
1 teaspoon vanilla bean paste
   or extract

Butter filling
100 g (3½ oz) unsalted butter,
   softened, plus extra for greasing
50 g (2 oz/generous ¼ cup)
   soft dark brown sugar
1 teaspoon ground cinnamon
100 g (3½ oz) toasted pecans,
   roughly chopped

Warm the milk and butter in a small saucepan until the butter has melted, then set aside.

Mix the flour, sugar, yeast, cinnamon and salt in the bowl of a stand mixer fitted with a dough hook. With the speed on slow, pour in the eggs, milk and butter, and mix until combined to form a rough dough. Turn the speed to medium and knead for 6 minutes until you have a soft, smooth dough. Cover the bowl with cling film (plastic wrap) and set aside to rise at room temperature for 1–1½ hours, until doubled in size.

To make the caramel, melt the butter and sugar in a pan, stirring to combine. Stir in cream, maple syrup, salt and vanilla. Bring to a simmer and bubble gently for 5 minutes, then remove from the heat and set aside to cool to room temperature.

When the dough has nearly doubled in size, lightly grease a 23 cm (9 in) square, deep cake tin (pan). For the filling, beat the butter, sugar and cinnamon together with a wooden spoon in a mixing bowl.

On a lightly floured surface, roll the dough out to a 35 × 40 cm (14 × 16 in) rectangle, then trim the edges so they are straight. Spread the butter filling all over the top, then sprinkle with half the pecans. Starting from one of the shorter sides, roll the dough up into a tight log. Trim the ends and slice into 9 pieces (use a lightly floured bread knife to divide it into 3 pieces before cutting each of these into 3). Place in the tin in 3 rows of 3 buns. Cover with cling film and leave to prove at room temperature for 45–50 minutes.

Preheat a fan oven to 160°C (320°F/gas 4).

Remove the cling film from the pan and bake for 25–30 minutes until golden. Take out of the oven and leave to cool for 5 minutes before lifting out onto a wire rack. Cool to room temperature before removing from the tin and tearing the individual buns apart. Set on a baking sheet and spoon the chilled caramel over the top, then sprinkle with the remaining nuts.

MAKES: 6
PREP: 20 mins
COOK: 25 mins

I love these little flourless cakes. They're made almost like a soufflé, so they puff up then sink when they come out of the oven, leaving a little crater in the middle that's perfect for piling up with sour or whipped cream and berries or nut brittle. I've also made them using roasted and ground hazelnuts for more of a praline-y flavour. The mixture can also be baked in a 23 cm (9 in) round cake pan, to make one large sunken chocolate cake – it may need 5 minutes longer in the oven though.

FLOURLESS CHOCOLATE CAKES

—

with sour cream and cocoa

175 g (6 oz) unsalted butter,
    softened, plus extra for greasing
200 g (7 oz) dark chocolate with
    at least 70% cocoa solids, chopped
5 eggs
175 g (6 oz/¾ cup) caster
    (superfine) sugar
½ teaspoon fine sea salt
100 g (3 ½ oz) ground almonds

To serve
sour cream or whipped double
    (heavy) cream
berries or chopped, toasted nuts
cocoa (unsweetened chocolate)
    powder (optional)

Preheat a fan oven to 140°C (280°F/gas 3). Grease the base of 6 × 10 cm (2½–4 in) cake tins (pans) and line them with baking parchment.

Melt the chocolate in the microwave or in a heatproof bowl set over a pan of barely simmering water, then set aside to cool slightly.

Separate the eggs, putting the whites in a mixing bowl and the yolks in a small bowl. Using electric beaters, whisk the egg whites until they form stiff peaks, then sprinkle over 75 g (2½ oz/scant ⅓ cup) of the sugar and whisk until stiff and glossy. Set aside.

In another large mixing bowl, use the electric beaters (there's no need to clean them after the whisking the egg whites) to cream the butter and the remaining 100 g (3½ oz/scant ½ cup) sugar for 3–4 minutes until pale and fluffy. Beat in the egg yolks, then the melted chocolate and salt. Use a spatula to fold through the ground almonds until combined.

With the spatula, stir one-third of the egg white into the chocolate mix to loosen it, then carefully fold in the remaining egg white in two additions, trying to lose as little air as possible, but ensuring they're completely incorporated. Carefully divide the mixture between the cake tins, gently smooth the top and bake for 20–25 minutes until set in the middle. Leave to cool in the pans, set on a wire rack.

Remove from the tins and top with sour cream or whipped cream, berries or nuts, or just a dusting of cocoa powder.

**SERVES: 8–10
PREP: 30 mins +
overnight chilling
COOK: 10 mins**

I learnt to make a raw version of this clever vegan tart while studying at Matthew Kenney Culinary in LA and I thought it was really impressive. The filling is only made of three ingredients (plus a little sea salt) and it tastes just so good. You can top the tart with crushed nuts as I have, or red berries are nice too. This quantity will also make 4–6 individual tarts in 8 cm (3 in) cases.

VEGAN CHOCOLATE HAZELNUT TART

California Living + Eating

Hazelnut tart crust
200 g (7 oz/1½ cups) whole blanched
   hazelnuts
2 tablespoons cacao powder
1 tablespoon maple syrup
3 tablespoons coconut oil, melted
pinch of fine sea salt

Filling
300 ml (10 fl oz/1 cup) maple syrup
12 tablespoons or 60 g (2 oz/½ cup)
   cacao powder
6 tablespoons coconut oil, melted
pinch of fine sea salt

Preheat a fan oven to 160°C (320°F /gas 4).

For the tart crust, tip the hazelnuts onto a roasting tray (pan) and roast for 8–10 minutes until golden, then remove from the oven and set aside to cool completely.

Set aside about 10 of the cooled nuts to garnish. Tip the remaining nuts into a food processor and blitz, pulsing until just finely ground, (take care not to over-blend or the nuts will release too much oil). Tip in the cacao powder and blitz again briefly until combined, then add the maple syrup, coconut oil and salt. Blitz until just combined.

Line a 20 cm (8 in) tart case with a large square of cling film (plastic wrap) and, using your fingertips, press the tart crust evenly over the base and up the sides (if your case is deep don't worry if it the crust doesn't quite reach the top of the sides). Smooth with the back of a spoon and chill for at least an hour.

For the filling, put the maple syrup in a mixing bowl and, with a balloon hand whisk, whisk in the cacao a little at a time (it's important you do this slowly or the cacao can cause the mixture to seize). Once combined, whisk in the melted coconut oil a little at a time until you have an emulsified mixture. Stir in the salt, then pour into the tart case. Chill overnight (or for at least 6 hours).

Just before serving, remove the tart from the case and remove the clingfilm. Roughly chop the remaining hazelnuts and scatter over the top.

California Living + Eating

I tried many variations of this recipe: adding walnuts, chocolate or poppy seeds, substituting half the plain flour for rye, and experimenting with alternative sweeteners like date syrup. They all produce a decent loaf, but the truth is I just like classic banana bread. Using buttermilk in the mix gives a very moist crumb. And the cracked sesame crust is optional. You can bake the loaf without it, though it is really quite delicious.

SERVES: 8–10
PREP: 15 mins
COOK: 1 hr

BUTTERMILK BANANA BREAD
—

with cracked sesame crust

80 g (3 oz) unsalted butter, melted,
 plus extra for greasing
150 g (5 oz/generous ¾ cup)
 soft light brown sugar
200 g (7 oz/1⅔ cup) plain
 (all-purpose) flour
1 teaspoon baking powder
½ teaspoon bicarbonate of soda
 (baking soda)
½ teaspoon fine sea salt
325 g (11 oz) very ripe mashed banana
 (about 3 medium-large bananas)
2 large eggs
80 g (3 oz) buttermilk

Topping
1 tablespoon golden caster
 (superfine) sugar
2 teaspoons toasted white sesame
 seeds (see method on page 25)

Preheat a fan oven to 150°C (310°F/gas 3); grease a 900 g (2 lb) loaf tin (pan) and line it with baking parchment (see Note on page 199).

Melt the butter in a small saucepan, take off the heat and stir in the sugar; set aside to cool while you measure out the flour, raising agents and salt. Mash the bananas in a separate bowl, using the back of a fork. Also mix the caster sugar and sesame seeds in a small bowl for the topping.

Using a balloon whisk, whisk the eggs in a large mixing bowl. Whisk in the butter and sugar, then the banana, then the buttermilk. Finally gently mix in the flour mixture (don't over-whisk, just mix until combined). Tip into the loaf pan, evenly scatter over the sugar and sesame topping, then bake for 1 hour until golden on top and a skewer inserted into the centre of the loaf comes out clean.

Remove from the oven and set aside to cool in the pan for 15 minutes, then transfer to a wire rack to cool completely.

California Living + Eating

**SERVES: 8–10
PREP: 15 mins
COOK: 30 mins**

Although I've called this cornbread, it's actually not so far from a classic polenta cake, using ground almonds as a soft textural contrast to coarse polenta. It's gluten-free (don't forget to use a gluten-free baking powder) and made entirely with honey rather than refined sugar, so it's slightly less sweet than most cakes, too.

BLUEBERRY + HONEY CORNBREAD

150 g (5 oz) unsalted butter,
  softened, plus extra for greasing
3 eggs, separated
150 g (5 oz) runny honey
200 g (7 oz) ground almonds
100 g (3½ oz/⅔ cup) quick-cook
  polenta (cornmeal)
1½ teaspoons baking powder
½ teaspoon fine sea salt
grated zest of 1 lemon
150 g (5 oz) blueberries

Honey butter glaze
20 g (¾ oz) runny honey
20 g (¾ oz) unsalted butter

Preheat a fan oven to 140°C (280°F/gas 3). Lightly grease a 20 cm (8 in) round cake tin (pan) and line it with baking parchment.

Get all the components ready: separate the eggs, putting the whites into a large mixing bowl and the yolks in a small bowl. Measure the honey and butter into another large mixing bowl, then measure the dry ingredients into a fourth bowl.

Using electric beaters, whisk the egg whites until they form stiff peaks, then set aside. Next, use the electric beaters (there's no need to clean them after whisking the egg whites) to cream the butter and honey together until light and combined. Beat in the eggs yolks, then the lemon zest, then fold the dry ingredients into the mixture with a spatula until just combined.

Finally, gently fold the egg whites into the cake mixture, trying to lose as little air as possible, but ensuring they're completely incorporated.

Tip into the cake tin, smoothing the top, then sprinkle over the blueberries. Bake on the lowest shelf of the oven for 45 minutes until golden and a skewer inserted into the middle of the cake comes out clean.

Just before the cake comes out of the oven, make the glaze by heating the honey and butter in a small saucepan until combined. When the cake is ready and out of the oven, pierce it with a skewer in any areas not covered by blueberries. Spoon the hot honey butter all over the top. Cool in the cake pan for 15 minutes, then remove and leave to cool to room temperature on a wire rack.

———

NOTES ON… SEPARATING EGGS
In more dense cake mixtures, like this one which contains no flour, or the Carrot and Coconut Cake on page 199, I often separate the eggs and whisk the whites separately to incorporate more air into the cake. You needn't be as vigilant as when making meringues, but make sure there's no fat in the bowl or on the beaters, or the whites won't whisk up. Start beating on a slow speed, then increase speed, and keep going until they just form stiff peaks (when you pull out the beaters).

WHERE TO EAT

I am by no means an expert on restaurants in California (Eater.com is my go to), but I have eaten at many places that inspired the recipes in this book. Generally I am most comfortable in casual, inexpensive eateries, so you won't find much fine-dining listed here though there is plenty to be had. I also mention only two farmers' markets, but there are many more worth seeking out.

—

SONOMA

Fig & The Girl – Longstanding rustic French-Californian bistro in downtown Sonoma with pretty patio dining. *thegirlandthefig.com*

Shed – Delightful market, café and community space in Healdsburg with exemplary Californian food, nicely curated homeware and a fermentation bar. *healdsburgshed.com*

Zazu Kitchen + Farm – Fun, seasonal and local restaurant at The Barlow, a large outdoor market in Sebastopol with cafés, shops and bakeries. *zazukitchen.com*

Willi's Wine Bar – The original Willi's was sadly lost in the 2017 wildfires, but at the time of writing there were plans to reopen it at a different site in Santa Rosa with a similar menu of small plates and local wines. *starkrestaurants.com*

—

SAN FRANCISCO + EAST BAY

Chez Panisse – From humble beginnings in 1971, Alice Waters' Berkeley restaurant is now widely recognised as *the* pioneer of California cuisine. Downstairs is a formal fixed-menu restaurant, upstairs is a smart café. Both offer beautifully pared-back Cal-Mediterranean cooking that takes pride in local, organic ingredients. *chezpanisse.com*

The Ferry Building – As well as tri-weekly farmers markets (Tues & Thurs 10am–2pm, and Sat 8am–2pm which is the biggest), The Ferry Building also houses numerous shops and restaurants. Don't miss Cowgirl Creamery for Californian cheeses and The Slanted Door for modern Vietnamese food. *ferrybuildingmarketplace.com*

La Taqueria – No-frills, counter-service burrito and taco bar. Order the carne asada burrito dorado-style. *2889 Mission St, San Francisco, CA 94110*

Nopa + Nopalito – Nopa has been serving inspired Californian cuisine since 2006 with all sorts cooked expertly on the wood-fired grill. Nopalito is its organic Mexican offshoot serving great tacos and ceviche. *nopasf.com, nopalitosf.com*

Outerlands – Thoughtful neighbourhood restaurant out on the west-side of the city, a few blocks from the ocean. Great brunches. *outerlandssf.com*

Pizzeria Delfina – Reliably good, blistered-crust pizzas. Try the salsiccia topped with housemade fennel sausage. *pizzeriadelfina.com*

Rintaro – Exciting Cal-Japanese cooking in a modern izakaya setting. *izakayarintaro.com*

Saul's Restaurant + Deli – Jewish deli just up the road from Chez Panisse in Berkeley. Drink roasted ginger soda and eat 'everything' bagels piled high with smoked salmon. *saulsdeli.com*

State Bird Provisions + The Progress – Buzzy sister restaurants and next-door neighbours. State Bird delivers Cal-Japanese dishes via dim sum trolleys, while The Progress serves family-style sharing meals. *statebirdsf.com*

Swan Oyster Depot – Oysters, seafood and sourdough served Monday-Saturday 10.30am–5.30pm. *swanoysterdepot.us*

Tartine Bakery + Tartine Manufactory – Join the queue at Tartine Bakery for the glorious morning buns and toasted sandwiches, or book at table at the Manufactory for elevated all-day dining. Both are situated in the city's Mission district and

California Living + Eating

offer ample opportunity to sample Tartine's highly prized sourdough. *tartinebakery.com*

Zuni Café – Opened in 1979 and still going strong, serving Cal-Mediterranean food from brunch to dinner. The brick-oven roasted chicken with warm bread salad is an essential San Francisco dish. *zunicafe.com*

CENTRAL COAST

La Super-Rica Taqueria – Famed family-run Santa Barbara taqueria known for its no-frills digs and authentic Mexican food. *622 North Milpas Street, Santa Barbara, CA 93103*

The Lark – Creative Californian cooking and great wine, set in a buzzing former fish warehouse close to Santa Barbara's beachfront. *thelarksb.com*

Nepenthe – Utterly breath-taking views of Big Sur are guaranteed at this restaurant/café perched 250m above the Pacific coastline. *nepenthe.com*

Thomas Hill Organics – Charming Paso Robles restaurant dedicated to showcasing the best of the Central Coast's food and wine. *thomashillorganics.com*

LOS ANGELES

Broken Spanish – Elevated modern Mexican food and cocktails in Downtown LA. *brokenspanish.com*

Erewhon – Ethical, sustainable grocer and café with an outstanding hot and cold deli counter and coffees and juice galore. *erewhonmarket.com*

Gjelina – Iconic Venice restaurant widely considered to be a pioneer of California cuisine. The menu is huge but everything is good, especially the veg section. Next door, GTA serves great takeaway coffee, slices of pizza and the best sesame sourdough in town. *gjelina.com*

Gjusta – Gjelina's sister bakery, deli and café with long queues at the counter for brilliant sandwiches, roasted meats and smoked fish. *gjusta.com*

Jon + Vinny's – Pitch-perfect pasta, pizza and salads in a relaxed modern Italian diner. Owners Jon and Vinny are behind several other must-visit LA restaurants: Animal, Son of a Gun, Trois Mec and Trois Familia. *jonandvinnys.com*

Kismet – Acclaimed Silverlake restaurant serving Middle Eastern food with a Californian outlook. Don't miss the broccoli toast. *kismetlosangeles.com*

Kogi Korean BBQ – Five trucks and a permanent taqueria serving outstanding Korean-Mexican fusion. The short rib tacos are a must. *kogibbq.com*

La Isla Bonita Taco Truck – No-frills truck that has been parking daily (12am–6pm except Thursdays) on Venice's Rose Avenue since the 80s. *400 Rose Ave, Venice, Ca 90291*

Lodge Bread – Exceptional sourdough and other baked goods. The shakshuka and the fat pita sandwiches are breakfast highlights. *lodgebread.com*

Malibu Farm Restaurant + Café – for a casual brunches overlooking the ocean. *malibu-farm.com*

Night + Market – Vibrant Thai food in three LA locations – Silverlake, Venice and Weho. *nightmarketsong.com*

Pizzeria Mozza – Great spot for wood-fired pizzas and chopped salads. *pizzeriamozza.com*

Plant Food + Wine – Utterly inspired vegan cooking in a romantic fairy-lit garden on Venice's Abbot Kinney. *matthewkenneycuisine.com*

Rose Café – Buzzing Venice bar, restaurant and café. The breakfast burritos are the best in town and the evening menu offers brilliant So-Cal cuisine and cocktails. *rosecafevenice.com*

Santa Monica Farmers Market – One of the state's biggest markets overflowing with Californian produce. Note that Wednesday and Saturday markets are at a different location to Sunday.

SAN DIEGO

Galaxy Taco – Colourful taco joint in La Jolla with great housemade blue corn tortillas. *galaxytaco.com*

California Living + Eating

ACKNOWLEDGEMENTS

BIG THANKS TO...

Nassima, without you this book wouldn't be. Your good nature, relentless hard work and mind-blowing talent have made this book more than I ever could have hoped for. You're a total star and I am forever grateful.

Linda, for your great eye and beautiful styling.

Jennie, I couldn't have got through that food shoot without you! You're brilliant, a dream in the kitchen and *the* best company on long car journeys.

Katie, I was so happy to have you work with me on this even very briefly! You're ace, always!

Maria, your hard work, smiles and knock-out morning coffee are always appreciated.

Kajal, thank you for allowing me this brilliant opportunity. I know how much hard work goes into a book behind the scenes and I'm grateful for all the time you have spent on it. You also brought together a great team: Claire for her design prowess, and Laura for her keen editing skills. And Emma, thanks for leading me the way to Kajal in the first place!

Ruth, thank you for helping me spread the word about the book. And thank you to everyone at Hardie Grant who had a hand in making this book come to life. I didn't meet you all, but I am so grateful.

Claudia, thank you for your calm, considered and always wise advice.

Gayle and Emma at Visit California, thank you so much for your help organising the location shoot for this book. It wouldn't be half the book it is without these shots.

All of the hugely talented California-based chefs who inspired these recipes, and all the people who took the time to talk to me about food and wine in California, especially Joyce Goldstein, Chad Robertson, Nikki Minton, Trey Foshee, Anna and Erik Olson, Damian and Amanda Grindley, Christian Vaughan, Ken Melban and Jessica Hunter.

The entire team at *Waitrose* magazine past and present, I loved working with you all on that magazine and you all taught me so much. Especially William. Your belief in me as a food editor and the confidence you instilled in me changed my career. I will be forever grateful for that.

All of my brilliant friends, thanks for your continued support and belief. But particularly those who selflessly helped me with the book. The testers: Amy, Gemma, Hannah, Lauren, Leanne (almost), Maisie, Marie, Navah, Rosie and Tom. The wordsmiths: Amy, Jess and Mark. George, for dressing me (kind of). Emily, for your ongoing advice on everything (and the loan of your gorgeous house!). And eternal thanks to you, Nav. You made your home in LA my home on so many occasions… I am so grateful and I couldn't have done this without your positivity.

Tom, you tasted everything in this book! Which was no mean feat. You also listened, supported and guided me unwaveringly throughout this process. And I will never be able to thank you enough for that.

To my family – Alice and Graeme, Adam and Kat, Geraldine, Eva and Katja – for our shared love of food.

Mum, you taught me to work hard and keep going. And that's how I got here.

Dad, this book is dedicated to you. I wish you could see it. I think you would have liked it.

California Living + Eating

ABOUT THE AUTHOR

Eleanor Maidment is a London-based food writer and stylist. From 2011-2018 she was the food editor of the multi award-winning *Waitrose Food* magazine, during which time she wrote, developed and edited recipes for its 2 million readers on a daily basis. She continues to write and style recipes for Waitrose, as well as contributing to numerous websites, books and magazines. She has worked as a chef, and spent many years on the editorial team at Square Meal restaurant guide and website, writing about chefs and reviewing restaurants, before attending Leiths School of Food and Wine in 2010 where she graduated with distinction. She has been interested in food and culture from an early age, and wrote her dissertation on the cultural inheritance of food while studying Social Anthropology at the University of Edinburgh.

She first visited California in the 1980s and fell in love almost immediately.

INDEX

California Living + Eating

Published in 2019 by Hardie Grant Books,
an imprint of Hardie Grant Publishing

Hardie Grant Books (London)
5th & 6th Floors
52–54 Southwark Street
London SE1 1UN

Hardie Grant Books (Melbourne)
Building 1, 658 Church Street
Richmond, Victoria 3121

hardiegrantbooks.com

British Library Cataloguing-in-Publication Data.
A catalogue record for this book is available from
the British Library.

California: Living + Eating by Eleanor Maidment

ISBN: 978-178488-245-7
10 9 8 7 6 5 4 3

Publishing Director: Kate Pollard
Commissioning Editor: Kajal Mistry
Art Direction: Claire Warner Studio
Photography: Nassima Rothacker
Photography Assistant: Maria Aversa
Cover Artwork: Richard Robinson
Food Styling: Eleanor Maidment
Food Styling Assistants: Jennie Vincent
and Katie Marshall
Prop Styling: Linda Berlin
Editor: Laura Nickoll
Proofreader: Wendy Hobson
Indexer: Cathy Heath

Colour Reproduction by p2d
Printed and bound in China by Leo Paper Group